MW01196304

In Praise of
Love Is the New Currency

Reading *Love Is the New Currency* gave me chills and resonated deeply with where I've been and where I have chosen to go on my own life journey. Linda is spot on in reaching a place in your heart that you cannot deny or move away from. *Love Is the New Currency* sheds light upon the notion that we don't need to have super powers to make an extraordinary difference in the lives of others.

> **Cyndi Laurin, Ph.D.**, author of the best-selling business titles *Catch!* and *The Rudolph Factor*

Love Is the New Currency is a heart opening book that quickly reminds us how interconnected we all are and how together WE can right the wrongs of the world. Beautifully written.

> **Ellen Marie George,** Amazon Power Reviewer, author, poet

In *Love Is the New Currency,* Commito has gathered the best of what makes us human and it's hard not to want to live up to it. These stories of encouragement, hope, and inspiration are a great read for anyone who doubts the power of a kind act.

> **Susan Richards,** New York Times best selling author of *Chosen by a Horse*

Love Is the New Currency is a must read for anyone who desires to live from their heart. While the stories are deeply touching, they go beyond mere emotion. They inspire you into action. Linda Commito has truly created a treasure that will expand your beliefs about the power of love!

> **Tom LaRotonda,** author of
> *The Four Elements of an Inspired Life: Accessing Practical Wisdom*

Love Is the New Currency is beyond moving. It's an extraordinary example of ordinary people putting others first. This book will fill you with hope and faith for the human race and inspire you to love more, dare more, and give more.

Andrea Costantine, co-author of
How to Bring Your Book to Life This Year

Love Is the New Currency is a powerful testament that each of us has the opportunity to touch other's lives and make a positive impact on the world. These stories will fill your heart with compassion and inspiration and may spark your own interest in finding a cause that you can embrace to help humanity. Yes, ordinary people can create extraordinary changes in the world through love.

Lisa Shultz, co-author of
Speaking Your Truth: Courageous Stories from Inspiring Women

Love Is the New Currency made me smile from ear to ear! In the same engaging style as *Chicken Soup for the Soul,* Linda Commito weaves inspirational stories about people we will never meet who may just change our lives. ... In a world choked by financial challenges, *Love is the New Currency* is a breath of fresh air.

Donna DeNomme, award-winning,
internationally published author of
Turtle Wisdom: Coming Home to Yourself and *Ophelia's Oracle*

My heart was touched and my soul was moved as I read these wonderful stories that truly capture the essence of the human heart. *Love Is the New Currency* is an enormously inspirational book that brings out the very best within us. You will be nourished and touched by these moving stories, filled with gentle wisdom that delivers a powerful message.

Frannie Hoffman, author of
From Modeling Clothes to Modeling Self

Love Is the New Currency contains refreshing perspectives and new insights, and creates boundless inner energy that the reader can feel building page after page. Amidst all the monumental shifts occurring in the world around us, Linda Commito exposes the innate beauty of our humanity and reignites our soul's ability to radiate it effortlessly every day. It reminds us how to create that wonderful human ripple effect which is unstoppable once we choose that first splash.

Zen DeBrucke, author of *The Smart Soul,* co-founder of "Smart Soul Academy"

Linda Commito has struck gold with *Love Is the New Currency.* This inspiring book shows that when we recognize and celebrate our connection with others, our lives—and our relationships— become rich with abundant health and happiness.

Diana Daffner, author of *Tantric Sex for Busy Couples*

During challenging economic and personal times, we sometimes forget to look at what's really important in life. *Love Is the New Currency* contains a treasure trove of inspirational stories, reminding us of the wealth we can share through loving acts of kindness. Linda Commito intuitively recognizes that our lives are filled with golden nuggets of immeasurable value, and tells her inspiring stories with that belief in mind.

Laurel D. Rund, poet, artist and author of *Emerging Voices*

In these times of monetary instability, *Love Is the New Currency* has created a heart-centered exchange rate! Let this book give you hope and faith in the global values of humanity.

Amber Wolf, Ph.D., writer and recording artist

I am so grateful for the beautiful way that Linda's *Love Is the New Currency* encapsulates the inspiring message that authentic love and generosity of spirit bring at this crucial historical juncture in our lives. These stories truly convey what makes up the greatest treasures of this world: love, sweet love.

Susann Taylor Shier, author of *Soul Reunion: The Return Home from Separation*

Love
Is the
New
Currency

Creating a New Measure
of Wealth

Linda Commito

Jacquie
and June —
Live
from your
♡   Linda Commito

Love Is the New Currency™ is a trademark of CorEssence, LLC

© CorEssence, LLC 2011

Love Is the New Currency™

Printed in the U.S.A.
Printed May, 2011

ISBN # 978-0-9844468-0-3

All rights reserved. No part of this publication may be reproduced, stored in or introduced into a retrieval system, transmitted in any form or by any means, electronic, mechanical, photocopying, recording, or otherwise, without prior written permission of the publisher and author.

Book cover design: Graphic by Manjari
with inspiration for woman dancer from Eve Margo Withrow

Interior and Layout Design by Greystroke Creative
www.GreystrokeCreative.com

Back cover photo: Diana Keck

This book is a compilation of real stories and anecdotes, which the author shares from her point of personal artistic creativity. In some instances, the names and places have been altered in an effort to honor those who wish to remain anonymous.

For information regarding permissions, write to:

CorEssence Publishing
P.O. Box 3216
Boulder, Co. 80307

This book is dedicated to my mother,
Theresa Commito.

With all my heart, I thank you for not only giving me the gift of life, but for celebrating that life every step of the way. Your belief in the goodness of people and your faith in a loving God have given me hope for a better world. You are my inspiration and beautifully embody the essence of Love Is the New Currency.

Table of Contents

Chapter One

Chapter Two

Chapter Three

Gifts of the Heart 53

Chapter Four

Empowerment 77

Chapter Five

Body, Mind, and Spirit: A Human Experience 105

Chapter Nine

Feeding a Passion 171

Chapter Ten

Energy of Giving and Receiving 187

Chapter Eleven

111 Ways to Express Your Kindness 207

Epilogue 221

Love
Is the
New
Currency

CorEssence
Publishing

Be the change you wish to see in the world.

– Mahatma Gandhi

Introduction

The world is shifting. Are you?

We are experiencing dramatic changes—in nature, the earth, our governments, our financial systems, religious and political foundations—but the biggest shifts may be happening within ourselves. Overwhelmed by years of negative news, most of us are uncertain about who and what we can rely on, who can make things better. Like Dorothy in *The Wizard of Oz*, we have discovered that there is no wizard behind the curtain to magically fix what is not working or provide what we need.

Unsure of what's still left of our foundations, we are realizing that we are the ones who must eventually pick up the pieces and move forward to build a new world for ourselves and our children. While we may not *yet* believe that it will be better than it once was, our values are changing, and what we create will be different. We are already making sense of our fear and loss by helping others directly, immediately, and often in our own neighborhood. And, as we may later discover, the shift to a world that is more loving, friendly, and connected will be one that is worth being a part of—a world we wouldn't want to trade for the one we used to have, even if we could.

Despite the angst and insecurity of these challenging and unstable times, I believe there is a positive shift in consciousness taking place. And it's happening on a personal level. We're taking a look at the "big picture" as we evaluate our lives: What do we love and appreciate? How and with whom do we choose to spend our time? What gives hope, meaning, and value to our life? How are we contributing to the lives of others? What do we stand for? How do we measure our success or worth?

I've often asked myself these questions. More than two years ago, during my morning meditation, I heard an answer: "Love is the new currency." The words deeply resonated, though at the time I didn't understand why I had been given this insight or what I was supposed to do with it. I only knew I felt compelled to unravel its meaning. This book is about that ongoing journey to discover what a new *currency of love* looks like, and how its hopeful message is altering our relationship to money and even more importantly, our relationship to each other.

Among my earliest memories about money are the times when my Italian grandfather, who earned extra income from gardening, would secretly drop silver dollars into my pocket. Even as a young girl, I knew they were special, and I loved feeling the weight of them. "Don't spend them," my grandfather would say ... and I never did. In fact, I've kept those silver dollars to this day, not so much for their intrinsic worth as for the feelings of love that they still hold.

Today, the "almighty dollar" has been diminished, along with our portfolios, and with fewer of those dollars in our pockets, our perceptions about currency and its value are changing. We're beginning to grasp that money is only one of our many resources. We have unlimited access to a *currency of love* that is far more valuable and long lasting than metal or paper.

Awareness like this doesn't always come easily or quickly, and sometimes it takes a trip down the road of despair to discover the true richness of life.

I'm reminded of September 11, 2001. In one powerful moment, our world stopped and we became one country, one people, united through tragedy. Volunteerism and heroism were esteemed as a new way of being in our catastrophically disrupted world. Eventually we went back to the everyday activities that mark our way of life, but it has never been quite the same.

The rug was yanked out from under us on September 11. Now, years later, in the midst of a different kind of catastrophe, we're feeling as though the rug has been inched out from under us in what has been an insidious erosion of our trust, confidence, and hope.

It's an *erosion* rather than an *explosion*. Whether yanked or inched out, our foundations are no longer what we thought they were, and we are left suspended, uncertain about where and in whom to place our faith. We've learned that we cannot rely on governments and corporations to rescue us. We feel abandoned, and yet, perhaps, we have abandoned ourselves.

This deficit of trust has given us a new bottom line: We need to take responsibility, not only for our own lives, but also for the lives of the people we love, and even for those around us who are unable to take care of themselves. The concept of "we," doing it together, is becoming more important than doing it all for "me."

In a continually shifting world, what we need is a *currency of love* based on compassion, cooperation and community. These challenging times are teaching us that our ability to give, receive, love, appreciate, and serve others brings happiness and meaning to our lives in ways that money and things never have, and never will, provide. We're redefining our worth and creating a new measure of wealth.

How would you answer the question: *Are you wealthy*? When I recently asked this question of three friends over dinner, I received resounding responses of "Yes!" "Absolutely!" or "Totally!" None of them use money as a yardstick of wealth: Patti, a massage therapist, believes that her abundance comes from her level of relatedness to life, people, and nature. Tom, a handyman and carpenter, says, "My measure of wealth is being able to do what I love and have people appreciate it." And Megaera clearly considers her wealth to be the creation of a community of friends who love and enrich each other's lives.

Another friend, Jessie, later answered this question by saying that while she has not gained the monetary wealth that some aspire to, she feels wealthy in her most valued asset—knowledge. She finds that her abundance comes from a deeper understanding of the world, and she's most enriched when she can "spend" her knowledge to promote the well-being of others and of the planet.

I've come to realize that wealth is how we choose to define it. Author Henry David Thoreau wrote, "Wealth is the ability to fully experience life." David Rubin, a friend of mine, says, "My greatest wealth is to have learned just enough from all my challenges to live what I call a 'winning life'—a life that's based on the richness of human interaction, and understanding that everything that happens to us can be a vehicle for creating value."

Values can vary based on our cultural beliefs. In the Pacific Northwest, there was a tribe, studied by anthropologist Franz Boas, called the Kuakiutl, who measured their wealth and status by what they gave away, not by what they had. Their acts of giving were part of the potlatch ceremony. At one time, wool blankets were their most valued currency, and later it was copper, but regardless of the chosen means of exchange, it was the person who gave away the most who was considered wealthy.

Giving in any form makes us feel rich. There's no set way to define our measure of wealth: our inner and outer resources, relationships, passion for creative expression, our happiness in giving and receiving ... We each have our own unique gifts and style, and what's important is finding what those are and then sharing them in the most joyful way that we can. It's what nourishes our soul.

"He who knows he has enough is rich," said Lao-tzu, an ancient Chinese philosopher.

When we are able to let go of our fears of lack and separation, we're realizing that we *are* enough, we *have* enough, and the greatest resource we have to give is ourselves—our knowledge, our time, our skills, and most important, our love.

Like many others who are experiencing uncertainty in these challenging times, I'm redefining what gives my life meaning from a broader, more altruistic perspective, looking at the ways I can contribute to the well-being of others. My quest has led me serendipitously to individuals whose heart-centered stories address the core questions: "What is loving, hopeful, and meaningful in your world? And what are you doing to create it?" As you read *Love Is the New Currency*, I think you will be deeply touched by the answers.

You are invited to meet everyday people, who are changing lives through ordinary and extraordinary acts of love and kindness and to discover ways that people are making a positive difference in their relationships, their workplaces, their communities, and more. Their stories can incite and inspire you to look for and to express your own *currency of love* and to be a part of the shift towards creating a world that is loving, friendly, kind, and connected.

The beauty and richness of this collection of stories is that it's just a microcosm of what's going on in our world. Every day, people are showing up for others in memorable, life-changing, and, thankfully, never-ending ways.

Ultimately, it's people like you and me, and our friends and neighbors, who give me hope for a better world. Who we are and what we do matters. We *are* the ones who are bringing about real and lasting change. Together we are creating a new measure of wealth, *a currency of love,* that can never be taken from us, and that will only increase in value the more it is shared.

One
Karma Bank

How people treat you is their karma;
how you react is yours.
— Wayne Dyer

What if you knew, without a doubt, that everything that you do, think or say creates a ripple effect, making a difference, not only in your life, but in the lives of others? People and cultures have long believed this to be true, and many traditions include this idea in their philosophies, for example, the concept of karma.

A contemporary notion of karma is that there's a cause-and-effect relationship between our actions and deeds and what happens to us. Simply stated, "You reap what you sow." What's compelling is that it's the intention behind the act that creates the positive or negative outcome. If you give from a loving heart—for the sheer joy of it, without any expectation of being acknowledged or getting anything back—you're making a positive contribution to what might be considered your "karma bank."

For instance, when my friend Joyce recently drove me fifty miles to the airport, she refused to accept any money for gas, saying "I just want to treat you." She didn't expect anything in return, and laughingly said, "I'm creating good karma."

Conversely, when you give out of an obligation, to cover a wrong deed, or with an expectation of receiving something in

1

return, it doesn't have the same, if any, karmic value.

Let's consider the positive manifestations of karma. You make a deposit through an act of kindness to help someone in need, perhaps a total stranger. The currency is simply that of love and generosity of spirit. The good feelings you experience are fulfilling in themselves. If there's a payback, it might be random and not necessarily in kind.

But there's more. Most givers say they receive far more than they give. Some add that wonderful people or things seem to just show up as a natural and synchronous part of their life. In fact, I've personally discovered that the more I practice *giving to give*, the more these synchronicities happen, as if by magic.

Like some people, you may have an almost implicit trust that when you require something, you'll be able to reach into your karma bank and have that need met. You may have used the phrase "I have good parking karma" just as a parking space opens up for you on a busy street, subtly indicating that the good things you've done are being repaid to you. This stems from the popular belief that "what goes around comes around."

While our karma bank might not keep an official record or score, it seems as though some omniscient presence has a magnificent sense of justice—and humor.

Creating Good Karma

Outside a local market, Tom noticed a man in the pouring rain, who was standing by his car with the hood up, waiting for help to arrive. Tom immediately offered his assistance, got the car started, and sent the man safely and gratefully on his way.

The following week, Tom was riding his bicycle over a half-mile-long bridge when he got a flat tire. Not having the right tools to fix it, he began to walk slowly toward his destination with his malfunctioning bicycle. A professional cyclist, fully outfitted in spandex, came cruising by, noticed Tom, and stopped to help. He said, "It goes against my grain to see a cyclist pushing a bike."

Tom thought, *I know the universe is helping me because I helped that guy last week.* The cyclist took off Tom's damaged tube, replaced it with a spare, and inflated it with his CO_2 pump. Tom was soon on his way and he didn't even get his hands dirty.

That's what I call a beautifully functioning karmic banking system!

Unexpected Returns

Things don't happen so much to you as they do for you.
— Colin Tipping

Derek believes in treating people well—the way that he wants to be treated. "I do good for the simple act of doing it," he said. "If you take pleasure in the act, don't question why, don't ask for rewards. The rewards and pleasures come from the act. Karma always rewards me." Especially, it seems, when it's least expected.

While remodeling homes he'd purchased, Derek was introduced to a group of Mexicans, including Raimundo and his two sons, who were available for construction projects. The man who'd made the introductions told him, "Don't give them any more money because they'll expect even more," but Derek always gave them extra for a job well done. He never asked them to do a job he wouldn't do himself. And when payroll was short, he managed to come up with the money somehow, even if it meant taking it from his own pocket.

The workers weren't used to being treated so well by a *gringo*, but over the next seven years, they developed a friendship and a level of trust and respect for each other.

One holiday season, Derek was totally down and out. In the real estate crash, he'd lost everything: his houses, his business, and his marriage. He felt as though his whole life had fallen apart. One day, Derek got a call from Raimundo and his sons, whom he hadn't seen in six months. They asked if they could stop by to wish him a "Merry Christmas," and drove almost an hour to see him. As they were leaving, they handed him a wrapped present, and told him to open it later.

When Derek opened his gift, he found a wallet—with $1,000 in it. "It brought tears to my eyes. I knew that it was a lot of money to them, and I was blown away that all three of them had wanted to do something for me."

Although he desperately needed the money, Derek phoned them: "You guys, I appreciate it, but I can't take this."

Daniel, one of the sons, replied, "Yes, we want to give this to you. We had a great year. You are a good man and have always helped us. You have treated us better than anyone else, like family. We want you to have this."

It's a gift that Derek will never forget.

♡ *What are your thoughts or beliefs about karma?*

♡ *Do you believe that there is a cause and effect relationship between your actions and what happens to you?*

♡ *Have you found that the good feeling you get when you do something to help someone is a reward in itself?*

♡ *What is your philosophy about giving to others in need, whether you know them or not?*

Paying It Forward

Carry out an act of kindness with no expectation of reward safe in the knowledge that one day someone somewhere might do the same for you.

– Princess Diana

The movie *Pay It Forward* introduced a unique concept. In the film, as part of his class project, a young boy decides to help three people. His only request is that each of them "pay it forward" by doing something to benefit three more people. Using a mathematical formula, he demonstrates to his classmates the exponential power of duplication: hundreds, even thousands, of people can be helped as a consequence of one kind act.

Paying it forward invites you to fulfill someone's need, whether physical, emotional, moral or financial, in advance, without acknowledgement or expectation of something in return. If there's a request, it's simply to pass it on. The hope is that this act of generosity will have an energy and life of its own.

There are many ways people can "pay it forward"—from simple gestures to sustaining "pay-it-forward-as-you-wish" experiments. The following stories validate that giving unexpected gifts can be so uplifting it creates a ripple effect, propelling others to pass on the good will.

Tollbooth Tender

On a drive to the Tampa airport, Charlie found an easy way to "pay it forward." As he paid his toll to cross the Skyway Bridge, he gave an extra dollar for the person behind him. The other driver eventually caught up to him, thanking him with a wave and a smile.

Giving is contagious. A few weeks later, after hearing Charlie's story, I was on my way to the same airport and decided I wanted to "pay it forward" too. I asked the toll collector whether this "pay it forward" experience was common, and he replied, "It's happened before."

It was fun and my curiosity was aroused. *Who was in the car behind me? How would it touch them to experience the unexpected kindness of a total stranger?* A few moments later, a vehicle from out of state sped up to pull alongside my car. A woman acknowledged me with a big smile and wave as she drove past.

On the way back, after picking up my parents, my dad was inspired to pay the toll for the vehicle behind us. That car, filled with what we guessed to be Asian travelers, passed us a few moments later, its smiling occupants nodding and waving enthusiastically as they drove by. What a cool introduction to our culture! And what a warm feeling we got from initiating it.

Lattés Laced With Good Will

At a well-known coffee chain, customers at various locations have been pleasantly surprised by "pay it forward" experiences, with patrons so touched that they continued the flow of generosity by paying for the next person in line ... and the next ... and the next. Contagious giving at its best!

During one holiday season, *The Seattle Times,* in an article by Christina Siderius, reported an amazing 24-hour cycle of giving at a Starbucks in Marysville, Washington, where almost 500 people not only paid for the person behind them in the drive-through line, but often put in extra cash. The spirits of those treated to peppermint lattés and mocha frappuccinos were greatly elevated, and the joy was passed on. The staff used the money that was left over to purchase toys to support a local toy drive.

A similar "pay it forward" experience took place at a Starbucks in Loveland, Colorado, a city known for its friendliness, where fifteen people in a row paid for the customer behind them. Gary Noyes described his experience and how he decided to carry on the good will gesture a few days later at a different location:

Three months ago, I pulled into the Starbucks drive-through in Loveland. As I reached for my wallet to pay for my coffee, the attendant said, "The people in front of you have paid for it." I was shocked, because I'd never had the "pay it forward" experience before. I decided I would pass it on.

A few days later, I was inside a Starbucks in Estes Park, Colorado, where there was quite a line of people waiting to be served. The man behind me became upset because he was waiting so long. *Here's my chance,* I thought, as I stepped out of the line and offered to let him go ahead of me because I had plenty of time to wait. I also paid for his order. He was nonplussed, but I could see a wonderful change in his spirit. It was truly a great experience for me.

Karma Kitchen

Imagine going out for Sunday brunch with a friend. You go to an inviting restaurant where you order from a menu with no prices. After enjoying a delicious meal served by the friendly wait staff, you are handed a check which reads $0.00 and a note: "Your meal was a gift from someone who came before you. To keep the chain of gifts alive, we invite you to pay-it-forward for those who dine after you. Have a lovely day!"

Welcome to Karma Kitchen!

Karma Kitchen was started in Berkeley, California in March of 2007 by several volunteers, including Viral Mehta and his wife Pavi. The founders wanted to inspire and seed a "gift economy," where gifts and services are given freely with no strings attached. The restaurant has prepared and served meals with love ever since.

Mehta says, "Karma Kitchen aims to support a cultural shift from consumption to contribution, transaction to trust, isolation to community, and fear of scarcity to celebration of abundance. By including those we don't know in our circle of giving, our hope is that we shift from a "me" to a "we" culture," says Mehta.

Run mostly by volunteers, Karma Kitchen has done so well that it has expanded to locations in Washington, D.C. and Chicago. To date, volunteers have contributed more than 25,000 hours at the various locations.

Not only has Karma Kitchen been able to sustain the project through donations, but they give any excess monies to "Bread for the Journey," a non-profit organization that supports neighborhood philanthropy and community projects.

Everyone, from guests to volunteers, loves being a part of this circulation of giving and receiving, not only in the meals they are sharing, but in their visit to the Kindness Table, where people take and leave offerings: from CDs, Books and DVDs to magazines and little gifts, all without a price tag and all full of love.

Even people who are not dining, but simply hear about the "pay-it-forward" concept, are eager to contribute. A cab driver, upon hearing about Karma Kitchen from the passengers he was driving to the Berkeley location, handed them money at their destination, and said, "Please, give this to the restaurant."

One visitor beautifully summed up his experience as he walked out the door: "You are the stuff rainbows are made of."

Karma Kitchen is now one of the highest-rated restaurant on Yelp (online reader reviews) in all of Berkeley—amazing how an all-volunteer crew can pull that off!

SAME Café (So All May Eat)

A slight variation of the theme, "pay-as-you-can," is a slowly expanding trend led by people like Libby and Brad Birky, who opened their non-profit restaurant four years ago in Denver, Colorado. Thanks to numerous volunteers and patrons, they have been self-sufficient during a time when many restaurants and businesses are failing. Their concept is being emulated by others who envision a world where all may be nourished.

Following is their story:

Libby Birky noticed the dollar bill on the floor one morning as she opened the door to SAME Cafe. "Did we drop this?" she wondered. And then almost every day for the next eight months, she was heartened by the sight of a single dollar bill that had been pushed through the slot in the door. (On the rare day when there was no dollar bill, there would be two the following morning). One evening, Libby was working late and caught a glimpse of the giver, a man in tattered clothes who surreptitiously walked away. Although she has not seen him since, a dollar still awaits her arrival each day.

At a restaurant where customers receive no bills, and there are no cash registers or credit-card machines, one never knows what to expect. "You get awed and shocked every day," says Libby. Although there's a donation box at the end of the counter, on one particular day, two of the volunteers discovered a $50 bill next to a used coffee cup. They told Libby that the only person who had sat at that table was "the scrawny street person who looked like he was wearing all of the clothes that he owned." Incredulous, Libby realized that even she gets to have her stereotypes broken down.

It was while volunteering at homeless shelters, that Libby and Brad became disenchanted with the poor quality of the food and the lack of connection that people in poverty were experiencing. Glad to be able to go to a restaurant for a good meal at the end of their day of volunteering, they realized that others didn't have that option or the luxury of eating healthy food. So the idea for SAME Café was conceived. It took five years and their life savings to manifest.

The Birkys created their "pay-as-you-can" restaurant in the heart of a transitional neighborhood, where people from all walks of life could eat a fresh, organic, "cooked from scratch" meal. "We want to offer a piece of dignity that everyone can have access to," says Libby. There's no pressure to pay. Guests can choose to contribute by making monetary donations, by sweeping the floors, or by doing dishes.

Libby had noticed a dramatic change in the second week of November 2008, when several companies, realizing the economy wasn't going to turn around quickly, laid off huge numbers of people. That's when the lunch-only restaurant went from serving 35 to 50 people a day—with average donations totaling $7 or $8—to serving 90 people a day, averaging donations of $2 to $3. Still, SAME Café was able to eventually pay back Libby and Brad's initial investment, and continue to support itself on the "pay as you can" honor system, thanks to the open-hearted generosity of numerous volunteers, local businesses, patrons, and individual donors.

Libby and Brad are grateful to offer a space and opportunity for others to eat well, and to freely give or receive help as they are able. Their *currency of love,* and the best part for Libby, is creating a community for such a diversity of people: single moms, teachers, elderly patrons, business professionals, and those without jobs or a place to call home—all seeing each other in a dignified way in a place where they feel like they belong. It has validated Libby's belief: "Humans are good. They do the right thing when given a chance."

♡ *Have you ever been a part of a "pay it forward" experience?*

♡ *How did that make you feel as the giver or the recipient? Did you continue to pass it on?*

♡ *What can you do to create your own pay it forward experience?*

Paying It Back

Do to others what you would have them do to you
— Jesus Christ (Matthew 7:12)

We humans have a generous spirit for the most part. I've discovered that most people want to give back or repay an act of kindness, and will often choose to reciprocate with a gift of equal or greater measure.

When we can't repay someone directly, as in the case of a gift from an anonymous donor, there lingers a deep desire to continue the flow of generosity by paying it back to someone else, often a total stranger.

Appreciation, kind words expressed at the right time, good deeds, or just focusing our attention on the needs of someone else, can make a difference and may even save a life—whether yours or the person to whom you reach out.

"Paying it back" can be a one-time occurrence as in a random act of kindness, or as enduring as a lifetime of conscious giving.

The following stories depict individuals who've found creative ways to reciprocate the loving kindnesses they've received—even if it takes years for the right opportunity to present itself.

Ongoing Acts of Giving

Massage therapist Ridley Hutchinson is a kind and compassionate man with twinkling eyes, a contagious laugh, and a sympathetic ear. When I initially asked him if he had any stories to share about how he was making a difference in the lives of others, like so many givers, he couldn't think of a single thing.

It was a while before I heard this story:

Ridley was stunned when his son, Ecta, was diagnosed with leukemia around the time of his fourth birthday. What followed were seven long, anguish-filled years of hospital stays and treatments. When Ridley first arrived at the Ronald McDonald House, where he spent extended stays to be near his son at the hospital, he said, "I felt like I had a ton of bricks on each shoulder." The support and comfort he received from the volunteers and staff there fostered a desire to someday pay back the kindness.

Ecta passed away at age 11. These many years later, Ridley has found a wonderful way to give back and to honor his son. Every Tuesday for the last six years, Ridley has driven thirty minutes each way to the nearest Ronald McDonald House to give free therapeutic massages to distressed parents, hospital patients, and others in need.

With a catch in his voice, Ridley recalled one particular patient: a young boy between twelve and fourteen years of age, who'd acquired a staph infection requiring the amputation of one hand, all of the fingers (except the thumb) on the other hand, and both of his legs below the knees. "I couldn't get this boy out of my mind, thinking how challenging it would be for him to get through his life with such obstacles," said Ridley. "When his caregivers brought him to me for a massage treatment, I felt grateful to be able to offer him some comfort."

♡ *Have you ever received something that so touched you that you wanted to reciprocate by doing something as wonderful?*

♡ *Did you pay it back directly or pay it forward to someone else?*

♡ *What are the ways that you most enjoy giving to others?*

♡ *How do you receive the kindness and generosity of others?*

Walking in the Shoes of Another

Never criticize a man until you've walked a mile in his moccasins.
– Native American Proverb

Several years ago, I took a workshop on accessing and developing intuition. I will never forget one of the exercises: All eighty of us were asked to remove our shoes upon entering the large conference room. Later during the session, we were asked to go to that entry, to put on someone else's shoes, and to walk around in them for ten minutes. We were then to write about our experience.

I was flooded with images of the well-worn shoes I'd selected and what their owner's life might be like. The next task was to find that person and to ascertain whether we had intuited correctly. Amazingly, many of our insights were spot on.

We all have access to an inner guidance system that helps us to tap into information that can be helpful to ourselves and to others. When we suspend judgment and tune in to someone from our heart awareness, it's easier to imagine what it might feel like to trade places. I must admit that at the end of the exercise, I was happy to put my own shoes back on—they had a familiar path of wear that I found comfortable.

Here are the stories of two people whose personal experiences made it easy for them to relate to another's challenging situation:

Mary knew what it meant to be in dire straits. She'd been on her own, caring for her five young children on a bus driver's salary while her husband was in prison. At one point, when she didn't know where the money for the next meal would come from, a Good Samaritan had come to her aid. Mary never forgot about it, and a couple of years later she found a way to give back.

Mary noticed that Bonnie, a woman in her church, was experiencing financial hardship. Reflecting on the Biblical passage about not letting the left hand know what the right hand was doing, Mary went to Roberta, another church member, handed her an envelope filled with cash, and asked her to give it to Bonnie without letting her know who the gift was from.

Bonnie, recently separated from her husband and raising two young children, broke down in tears when she received the envelope. "I can't believe that someone would want to help me."

Knowing that Mary gave from what little she had for herself and her own family, Roberta's heart was touched. She said, "It made me realize that, even in the midst of these tough economic times, we could all be more aware of other people and their difficulties. No matter how little we think we have, we can still reach out and help others with whatever it is that we can give. We never know when we could be walking in those very same shoes."

In another part of the country, Jane, a massage therapist, was working in a chiropractor's office when she met Denise, who was receiving treatment after a car accident. During one of her scheduled visits, Denise confided in Jane: "I've just moved to town with my son, who's handicapped. We're living in a hotel room and they've just increased their rates. I don't have much money and I'm afraid we might be living on the streets soon."

Jane remembered what her mother had taught her: "Put yourself in someone else's place and ask yourself '*What would I want someone to do for me?*'"

Even though she barely knew Denise, Jane suggested, "You can stay with me. I only have one bed, but I can offer you floor space."

With the purchase of an additional bed, Denise, her son, and their dog moved in with Jane for two months. Through Jane's generosity, Denise got a loving home for her family, as well as the opportunity to save enough money to rent a suitable place of her own.

Jane's invitation was the beginning of what became a beautiful, long-lasting friendship.

♡ *How do you express compassion for those in distress?*

♡ *Do shared experiences make it easier for you to reach out with kindness to someone else?*

♡ *What would you have done if you were Jane?*

Finding the Light

> *The best way to find yourself*
> *is to lose yourself in the service of others.*
> – Mahatma Gandhi

Lane and his wife look like they just stepped out of the pages of *Glamour* magazine. Deeply in love, they are first-time parents to a happy and healthy baby boy. An observer would never guess that Lane has lived anything but a charmed life.

For years, I had heard about Lane through his dad, who is a good friend of mine. Tomas had confided in me that it was difficult to watch his son struggling with addictions throughout much of his life. I didn't know the extent of those struggles until I had an opportunity to meet and talk with Lane himself.

In his own words, Lane shares his personal story, which took place a few years ago:

It was yet another futile attempt to run away from myself. Being a full- blown, active alcoholic, I couldn't stop drinking. I kept coming up with one more bright idea, and that usually involved going to another town, a new place, where no one would know me, and where I could start fresh. However, no matter where I went, within two weeks, "I" would show up, and all hell would break loose. Within days, I would find myself surrounded by the same people, just with different names.

My last attempt at a geographical cure took me over two thousand miles, from Dallas to Oregon, and within a few days, I found myself hand-cuffed and on my way to prison for two full years. It was not the first time I awoke to find myself behind bars.

Upon arrival at the maximum-security prison, dark and depressing, the smoke clearing as the booze wore off, I finally got in touch with the terrible, deep-seated loneliness that I had been trying to escape from all of my life.

In a concrete six-by-nine, two-man cell, many miles from friends and family, I met my "cellie," a Spanish guy who spoke very little English. We were so different that I felt even more disconnected and lonely.

As crazy as it might sound, the words to the song "It's Just Another Day in Paradise" kept running through my head. *Could there really be someone living in Maui or some island paradise who feels as miserable as I do? Are there actually people in prison who can envision themselves in paradise? Is it really all just a state of mind?*

A few days later, I was in a very deep depression. The only way out that I could come up with was to do away with this self that I couldn't seem to escape. I knew I was considered "government property," and that any suicide attempt needed to be successful or I would suffer dire consequences—namely "the hole," a cold, damp, steel room in solitary confinement—and I didn't want to find out if I could survive that.

While I was contemplating the best way to go about this, my cellmate, Juan, approached me with a letter he'd received from his girlfriend on the outside. I spoke practically no Spanish, but I understood from his broken English and creative sign language, that he was asking me to help him write a letter to his girlfriend to let her know he was okay and that he loved her.

Although I was consumed with self-pity and remorse, I reluctantly decided to take a few moments to help him out. We began at 6 p.m., right after dinner. The next thing I knew, there was a guard coming by the cell for the midnight count.

A second in prison feels like a minute, a minute feels like an hour, and an hour like a day. Somehow six hours had passed, and during those moments, I had perfect peace. I was free.

During the following two years, there were many people who didn't give up on me, especially my family and people at the AA meetings. They loved me until I could love myself. Through *A Course in Miracles* and the twelve-step program, plus a lot of soul searching, I learned many valuable lessons, forgiveness being the greatest of those.

And I've never forgotten how such a small act of kindness like writing a letter for another could be transforming, even in such harsh conditions. A little love went a long way and was a bright light in a very dark place.

Lane is now living the life he previously could only dream about. While enjoying personal and financial success, Lane gives back by volunteering at a local prison, an activity for which he had to undergo intense scrutiny. "When they took me to prison before, they weren't being so picky," he jokes.

He regularly shares the Twelve Steps with inmates to offer hope, and to give them a hand out of their own black hole. He sponsors some of the guys, who've completed their sentences and are ready to re-engage in society. He's especially proud of one man, now a friend, who has not only stayed sober, but is getting married and will be a father soon.

Speaking of proud, Tomas is thrilled to witness Lane's transformation, particularly the way in which he has become a good dad. Friends and family recently helped Lane celebrate a major accomplishment: three years of sobriety. And he's working on fulfilling another dream. He's writing a memoir with the intention of creating a piece of work that can help others.

Lane never forgets what it feels like to be on the other side of his luck, and he knows firsthand what it means to live on the street. "I don't have any grand illusions," he says. When someone asks for money, I don't judge the person or assess their need. It's real for that person, and it takes a lot to be able to stand there and ask for help. I can't turn down another's request."

He just reaches for his wallet.

♡ *Have you ever been in a state of depression?*

♡ *Who or what helped you to get out of that dark place?*

♡ *Are you able to reach out to others who feel hopelessly trapped in despair and are in need of support? How?*

Random Acts of Kindness

You cannot live a perfect day without doing something for someone who will never be able to repay you.

— John Wooden

What a delight it is to participate in random acts of kindness, whether as the giver or as the receiver. The air of secrecy, spontaneity, and surprise is refreshing in a world that tends to measure and calculate every decision and action.

Marisa worked in a large government office. Despite her personal struggles and depression at the time, she noticed that one of the secretaries, Betty, was ostracized to the point that another secretary asked to have her desk repositioned, so that they wouldn't have to see each other. A bit eccentric, Betty wasn't welcomed by her co-workers to join them for lunch or any other social activities. She kept to herself most of the time.

Identifying with the feelings of isolation, Marisa decided to lift Betty's spirits each day by leaving a little surprise on her desk, usually a candy bar, snacks or a card. She would secretly watch as Betty walked up to her desk, and with an inquisitive but delighted expression, looked around to see who might have left this sign of caring.

Although today, Marisa would be able to take it a step further and invite Betty to lunch, at the time, it was all she could do to notice and attempt to alleviate another's discomfort in a subtle and simple way.

Gradually, she noticed that Betty seemed happier as she came into work each day. And while Marisa never told where the treats were coming from, her spirits were lifted too. She learned a valuable lesson that has always stayed with her: The best way out of one's sadness or despair is to practice acts of kindness.

In each of the following stories, someone witnessed a visible need and chose to favorably affect the outcome of another's experience.

Generosity in a Plaid Shirt

C.T. Mills grew up in my small hometown. Although I'd heard her name mentioned, we never met until decades after I'd grown up and left home, when I returned for a class reunion. We felt an instant connection and only later discovered that we knew many of the same people and places.

When I mentioned that I was writing *Love Is the New Currency*, C.T. shared this next story about her encounter with a serial perpetrator of random acts of kindness:

One noon, my sister and I took Dad to lunch at a popular local restaurant in Sturbridge, Massachusetts, which, as usual, was packed. We ordered and ate well, but when we asked for the bill, our waitress nonchalantly said, "Oh, that was paid for already."

"What? This must be a mistake."

"Nope, no mistake. The guy with the plaid shirt, sitting at the counter, bought your meals."

"Why?"

"Don't know why. But he comes in for lunch every day during the week and buys someone their lunch every time."

When I went to thank him, he was already gone.

Over a period of nine months, the man paid for our lunch two more times. I caught up with him one time, as he was leaving, to say thanks. "You're welcome," he replied shyly. He then walked to his car, a faded blue Toyota Corolla, and drove off.

In this day and age, when good deeds typically carry expectations, I was fascinated by this unpretentious man. So when the opportunity arose, I asked one of the waitresses about him. His name was Tim, and he was married with children. She assured me that he wanted nothing in return: It simply made him feel good.

So taken by his generosity, I made a sizable donation to a food bank in his honor. Kindness is infectious. Tim has since moved out of the area, so people have to pay for their own meals these days, but his kind spirit still lingers in the air.

♡ *Have you ever been the recipient of a stranger's unexpected act of kindness?*

♡ *What was that experience like for you?*

♡ *In what ways has that affected the way you express your kindness now?*

A Story of Faith

I discovered a virtual gold mine of inspiring stories when I attended a meeting of eighty volunteers who were looking for ways to contribute to their community. It was there that I met Dee Walker.

Dee makes serving others a regular part of her life. For more than fifteen years, she has volunteered at Emma Booker

Elementary School, made famous when former President George H.W. Bush was filmed reading to the children on 9-11. The school is located in the poorest, almost totally minority community of Sarasota, Florida.

Dee shared this story about a time when she passed up an opportunity to help someone, and how she later rectified it. It reminded me of how often I am distracted or rushed and don't notice someone in need, and how little things can make a huge difference.

Told in her own words, here is Dee's story:

I saw them for the first time last week, walking away from the school where I was volunteering. The tall, young mom with an infant tucked under one arm and a toddler, no more than thirteen or fourteen months old, walking behind her, holding an empty bottle and struggling to keep up. I thought about stopping to help. I didn't. All that day, I regretted my decision, and promised myself that if I should ever see her again, I would give them a ride.

One morning, there she was again at the admissions desk, signing in her first grader, who had missed the bus. From wherever she lived, she had walked her daughter over so that she wouldn't miss a day of school. And there, crooked in her arm was the same infant, and at her feet was the same toddler. "Let me give you a ride home," I offered. "It's hot, and you and the babies must be tired." She nodded and thanked me. We drove quite a distance to her cousin's home. "Don't you have a stroller?" I asked. She shook her head no.

I was concerned about the state of the children, especially the toddler, with his ragged shirt, soiled diaper and dirty slippers. Both little ones held empty bottles. But I remembered that she had cared enough to get her first grader to school that morning. "I'll bring you a stroller," I told her. She smiled. Her life had probably been full of empty promises. Why should she believe this would be any different?

After dropping them off, I immediately drove over to Mothers Helping Mothers, located nearby. I knew that I would find a stroller. I didn't doubt it for one second.

I walked in and there it was—an almost new stroller, big and wide, with a comfortable, cushioned seat, a big basket underneath, and a large top to keep the sun off of the babies. Within five minutes, it was in my car and I was heading back to find the young mother.

While driving to her home, I saw her walking, pushing a small broken stroller.

I tooted the horn and stopped the car. "Where did you find that?" I asked.

"It was over by the trash can," she said.

"Let's try this one instead," I told her as I pulled the one I had just purchased out of my car. We put the dirty, broken one back by the trash can, and placed the babies in the secure and comfortable carriage.

She started to leave with her little ones, who were holding the same empty bottles, but she was heading to a nearby store. "Do you have money for juice?" I asked, and she nodded yes.

"You send a note with your first grader if you need anything else. Her teacher will find me."

This time she smiled, and this time I think she believed my words.

♡ *Have you ever walked or driven by someone who looked like they needed help, but you didn't stop because you were pressed for time?*

♡ *Was there a lingering thought or feeling about the missed opportunity?*

♡ *Today, allow yourself to slow down long enough to notice those around you.*

♡ *Say or do something kind for someone just to brighten their day.*

Good Samaritans

Love your neighbor as yourself.
— Jesus Christ (Matthew 22:39)

The phrase "Good Samaritan" is so commonly used that it's listed in the dictionary.

It comes from a compelling parable told by Jesus in response to a lawyers' question, "Who is thy neighbor?"

> While on a journey, a man is beaten, robbed, and left by the side of the road to die. Many pass him by, including those of his own tribe, and some even go across the road to avoid him. No one offers to help until a despised Samaritan stops to assist him and takes him on his donkey to a nearby town. Not only does the Samaritan secure a room and food and nurse him through the night, he pays for another two nights, and offers the innkeeper extra should there be a need before taking his leave.

Jesus asks, "Who was the good neighbor?"

Such munificence to a total stranger, and to one who might have looked down on him under other circumstances, is remarkable. The Samaritan generously treated the stranger as though he were a friend, and set a standard for compassion that was passed on for more than two thousand years.

In today's culture, given the Internet, cable television, and easier access to travel, the faces of our neighbors have changed. Or do we still consider "neighbors" to be only those who live near us, or who are members of our church, club or social circle? What about the objectionable person in need, who just happens to show up in our lives? Are we as apt to extend our love and compassion?

One evening at a popular local dance club, I chatted with two women, Melissa, to whom I'd recently been introduced, and her friend Bonnie. When I mentioned that I was collecting stories of everyday kindness, Melissa nudged her friend and said, "Tell her what you did to help that man." Apparently, it was a story that had been shared with only her closest friends and it took some convincing for Bonnie to tell it, with the stipulation that all names be changed.

The following story is a modern-day version of *The Parable of the Good Samaritan.*

Saved by the Kindness of a Stranger

Have you ever done something that wasn't part of your usual routine, but there was a prompting—a voice in your head or a feeling in your gut—that you simply couldn't ignore? You may have felt led to a particular person or place or asked to participate in an event. Whether the results were inconsequential or life-changing, you may have realized later that this was exactly what was supposed to happen.

One morning, Bonnie decided to go out for a cup of coffee and a newspaper, something she rarely does. The coffee shop was out of newspapers, but she spotted a free-standing newspaper box across the street and walked toward it.

There, lying on the ground, she saw what appeared to be an elderly homeless man, filthy, disheveled, and smelling so badly of urine that it was difficult to get close to him. In fact, several people made a wide circle around him as they walked by.

As Bonnie approached, she noticed that the man's lips were blue. He seemed disoriented.

"It looks like you need help," she said. He answered affirmatively.

Bonnie felt a moral obligation to help him: "I just had to. It was the only Christian thing to do." And without a second thought, she put him in her car, drove him to the nearest hospital, and waited with him until a doctor could check him out. "You're an angel," the doctor told her "and have most likely saved his life."

Bonnie left the man in the care of the hospital staff and went on with her day. She later received a phone call saying, "Sam's ready to go home."

"But I don't even know him," she replied.

"You're the only person we know to call."

What to do?

Bonnie drove back to the hospital to pick up, "Sam" with no idea of where this *ride home* would take her. Expecting to follow his directions to a local shelter, she was totally shocked to end up in an exclusive neighborhood.

She learned then that Sam, at 83, had just flown 1,000 miles on his own to visit his girlfriend. Upon his return, he had become disoriented and distressed.

Through subsequent conversations, she discovered that Sam was a retired businessman, who was well accustomed to the finer things in life. He was also lonely, and coming to the realization that, with his heart condition, he couldn't do things by himself anymore.

Sam was so touched by Bonnie's kindness and unwavering determination to help him, a total stranger, that he later offered her a job as his personal assistant. Bonnie was grateful that she could continue to make a difference in the life of the man she had saved.

- ♡ *In what way have you been or would you choose to be a Good Samaritan?*

- ♡ *What are your limits in terms of safety or your comfort zone? What would you have done if you were Bonnie?*

- ♡ *Have you ever made a judgment about someone, only to realize later that you were dead wrong?*

Angel in Disguise

Many people believe that angels come in various forms, including those disguised as humans, who show up at just the right time to offer guidance or even to save a life. Still others believe that angels sometimes express themselves through "whisperings."

I can attest to both through my personal experience:

One July Fourth weekend, at dusk, I was driving my four-wheel-drive vehicle, which was filled with food, clothes, and my big German shepherd. Since I don't drive well in the dark and was eager to get to my weekend getaway, I was driving faster than I should have been in the passing lane on a busy highway.

Suddenly, out of nowhere, I heard a voice tell me to "Slow down and move into the right lane." I responded immediately and moved over into the next lane just as my right rear tire exploded and shredded into pieces. Because I'd reduced my speed, I was able to safely move over to the shoulder of the highway and stop the car. I was shocked, realizing that if this had happened just moments before, I could have been seriously injured or killed.

Without a cell phone and not being near a house or an exit, I watched the sky getting darker, as I wondered how I was going to get to my destination.

I had stood by the side of my vehicle for fifteen minutes when a huge Safeway truck pulled up. Somehow, it was comforting to know that whoever this was worked for a local supermarket chain. A young man wearing a pink shirt got out of the truck and asked if I needed help. Boy did I ever!

The young man, Larry, located the spare tire and, eventually, found the jack, well-hidden under the rear seat. After pumping up the car, he realized that it wasn't high enough to allow him to put the tire on. Together, we searched along the side of the deserted highway for something to put under the jack to give it a lift, and were astonished to find some broken pieces of Formica. Amazed at our good luck, we gathered several pieces and stacked them. It was the perfect height.

When I offered to pay Larry for his time and effort, he refused, saying, "I believe that what goes around comes around."

After thanking him, I watched Larry drive off, leaving me with a new way to think about Safeway … SAFE WAY!

And I was convinced that there was an angel in a pink shirt driving to Wyoming.

♡ *Have you ever heard a whispering or a prompting to do something?*

♡ *If so, how did you respond and what were the results?*

♡ *Have you ever discovered that your act of kindness toward someone was a response to their prayer?*

Two
Universal Heart

If one completes the journey to one's own heart,
one will find oneself in the heart of everyone else.
— Father Thomas Keating

We are not alone. We are interconnected. We just happen to be living in separate bodies. We're united in a way that has nothing to do with the blood that runs through our veins, but rather the life energy that is within each of us. We're learning that turning away from our fellow human beings is like turning away from ourselves. Now, more than ever, we need to be there for each other.

I admit that there have been times when I'd thought about opting out—going to a place where I could live a simple, stress-free life. Once, while at a small dinner party, I asked my fellow diners, "Where would you go to get away from the chaos?" One man looked at me and simply pointed to his heart. He reminded me where I need to live to feel safe, connected, and at peace.

Whenever I feel a sense of belonging, either to people I love or as part of a community, I am happier, more hopeful, and without fear. Once I had the privilege of seeing the Dalai Lama "with 5,000 of my closest *friends*." Normally wary of being in a large crowd, I felt such a sense of connection and well-being I knew that if a bomb dropped right then, I would experience serenity.

Many of us experienced a unity with our fellow citizens after planes crashed into the World Trade Center in 2001. I remember being glued to my television set, alongside the man I'd hired to put in my patio, as we watched the twin towers collapsing. Through tears, we hugged each other, incapable of doing anything else but to witness the plight of our countrymen and our country's unfolding loss. That sense of connection is what it's supposed to be like. Why does it take a crisis or natural disaster to remind us of the *oneness* of which we are all a part?

We create a *currency of love* when we consciously cultivate that feeling of belonging every day. We embrace our oneness when we notice and include everyone everywhere, when we let go of the judgments and criticisms that make others feel isolated, and when we celebrate our differences, as well as our commonality. It starts with a journey to our own heart, from which we can begin to experience a universal heart connection to all beings.

World Family

*The same stream of life
that runs through the world
runs through my veins.*
– Rabindranath Tagore

In a small New England town, I grew up with my extended Italian family in a six-family house. On one side, my grandparents and uncle lived on the first floor, my aunt and her family on the second floor, and my parents, two brothers and me on the third floor. Across the railing, on the other side, were my cousins. It was like a "little Italy." We never lacked family members to be with and you were accepted just because you shared the same bloodline.

When I was in my twenties, my husband and I lived in London for a year while he attended graduate school. It was my first time away from a supportive system of family and friends. Toward the end of that year, while still abroad, my husband and I separated. I was left to work through feelings of loss, and to find a temporary place to live.

Upon learning of my circumstances, one British family whom I'd befriended said, "Our daughter is going away to college and we have an empty room. Why don't you stay with us?" I gratefully accepted, and it was as though there was no void for any of us. I became a part of their family, a surrogate daughter, even to the point of people mistaking me for their biological one. Ironically, a year later, when their son Kevin visited the United States and stayed with my parents for a few days while my brother was away, a similar thing happened—people thought that Kevin was their son.

The concept of a *world family*—the notion that we can have brothers, sisters, parents, children, cousins, aunts, and uncles everywhere—became a natural way for me to think and to live. This outlook was reinforced when, a year later, I once again left my birth family in Massachusetts and moved 1,900 miles away to Colorado.

I remember saying goodbye to my four grandparents, wondering if and when I would see them again. Once settled in Boulder, I volunteered to visit residents of a retirement home. What an opportunity! I soon found two of the most wonderful "grandmothers" and had the pleasure of visiting them weekly for many years. I realized that while I couldn't be with my own grandmothers, I could be with someone else's. I even got to be a part of *Grandma Anna's* 100th birthday celebration.

I didn't grow up with a sister to share things with, but my world has been blessed with loving "soul sisters," as we like to refer to ourselves. And I have many friends who are family to me.

One of these friends, Carol Kelly, was the only person that

I knew in Boulder, Colorado, prior to my move there. I had met her for all of fifteen minutes while she was visiting in my home town, and she invited me to call her when I arrived in Colorado. The Kellys—Nick, Carol, and their children, Silbi and Brian—*adopted* me, becoming my "Colorado family." I spent most holidays and special occasions with them for the next thirty years. That connection reinforced my belief that I don't need biological ties to define my concept of family … and that, at any age, I'm still adoptable.

Silbi, now grown and a mom herself taught me that there's a maternal instinct in mothers, one that makes the support and care of all children as important as their own. She believes "it is not about *my* child but about all children."

This is Silbi's story and vision of a one world family.

Global Mom

Giving is not about being able to afford to do it—
it's about deciding it must be done.
– Silbi Kelly Stainton

Sometime during the winter after her fifth birthday, Silbi was riding around Boulder, Colorado, with her parents, when she noticed that the huge star that always shone brightly on Flagstaff Mountain during the holiday season was still lit up long after its usual time. She asked her parents why. When her mother explained that it was going to remain lit until some Americans, who were held hostage in Iran, were let go, Silbi asked, "Why are they being held?" She became intrigued with the nightly news, unusual for a five-year-old, and still remembers watching the ticker-tape parade when the hostages were finally released. As years passed, Silbi developed a deep interest in a region of the world that seemed exotic and mysterious.

"I grew up in a home where public service was normal and

where people of all countries, cultures, and generations were respected and valued," said Silbi. "My parents were not driven by making a lot of money, but by doing good. They encouraged me and my brother to think about others and to be caring and compassionate people." The fact that her Irish-American parents came from opposing Protestant and Catholic backgrounds, and were able to disagree on many things, but coexist peacefully, gave her an enlightened perspective on conflict.

By the time she was in college and then graduate school, studying international affairs and counterterrorism, Silbi came to realize that the West had a wide communication gap with much of the Muslim world. All of this only served to fuel her passion and eventually lead to her life's work: expanding the educational and economic opportunities for children and their parents in places like Pakistan and Southwest Asia.

Silbi, now a mom herself to a three-year-old son and five-year-old daughter, explained, "Having children gave me the extra push to do something. When you become a mother, you become this person who is a mother of all children. When you hear of another child who is hungry, hurting, or in need, you just want to do something to help. It has inspired my vision to live in and create a world where the ability to eat, to attend school, to have access to clean water, and to be sheltered doesn't depend on where one is born."

With the support of her entrepreneurial husband Tim, Silbi was encouraged to act on her own and not to rely on the government to make things happen. She created a nonprofit organization, the Marshall Direct Fund, whose mission is to improve relations between the West and the Muslim world by working together to alleviate poverty and illiteracy.

Blond, with light eyes and fair skin, Silbi wears a dupatta (a long rectangular scarf) when she goes to Pakistan twice a year, for ten days at a time. In a country where more than 60% of the population lives on less than $2 a day, she sets up schools in impoverished areas, where the students are provided a free meal—for many the only meal that they will eat during the week. Founded in 2007, there are already 200 children attending these schools—children whose lives will be changed forever because they are learning to read and write. These schools also encourage the youngsters to be productive and confident citizens, and to ask "why" questions.

In one remote village, Silbi met two beautiful girls, ages ten and eight, with pale eyes and dark complexions, who were new to the area. They had been taken in by relatives after their parents had been killed. She says, "They looked at me with such hope and said in their native tongue: 'Please don't forget about us.' Whenever I feel burned out and exhausted, the memory of their sweet faces haunts me and I think, *If they can survive all that and still smile and be a help to their families, then I can do whatever I can too.* These and other children that I've met are like my own children. I think of them often, worry about them, and strive every day to give them opportunities to make their lives healthy, productive, and happy. Education offers the best chance for change."

Silbi finds it exciting to see communities become empowered and fight for their schools. And she loves it when fathers stand up for their daughter's right to teach or to learn. She smiles when she talks about the thirteen-year-old girls who tell her that they want to learn about computers, even though most have never seen one. Some share their dream of becoming veterinarians.

Although she loves the children, Silbi's favorites are the mothers and grandmothers, who are loving and hospitable. She recalls one grandmother, who was in her sixties but looked at least eighty. "When she saw me, this woman clasped her deeply lined hands around my face and began to cry. She hadn't seen a white-skinned person in eight years and wanted me to know that the Pakistani people love Americans and don't want to hurt us. 'Please come back,' she pleaded." Then this woman invited Silbi to her home, located in a slum, where she had an extended family of ten living in two rooms with no running water, and offered her the last bit of rice that she had. Like a mother feeding her child, she insisted Silbi eat it even though that was all she had to eat herself.

"It is men and women like these who have changed my life and won my deepest respect. How could someone with so little give everything? What is meant by 'poverty' when so many of the poor possess such a wealth of decency, hospitality, and generosity of spirit?"

Silbi believes size doesn't matter in philanthropy and charity. "What's important is for each of us to do something." All great change in the world has begun with a single person's acts. When these actions gain momentum, they turn into larger movements. Silbi says, "I listen to the part of myself that tells me to give because I know that giving is not about being able to afford to do it —it's about deciding it must be done."

The legacy continues. "At five years of age, my daughter is already a little public diplomat, telling her friends that her mom is going to Pakistan," says Silbi. Extremely compassionate, the little girl recently took her new tricycle to her mom saying, "I want to give this to the children in Pakistan." And when asked what she would like to be when she grows up, without hesitation she replies, "I want to be like my mommy and help poor children."

♡ *Do you have children of your own? If so, do you feel a deeper connection and understanding of other people's children, regardless of where they are from?*

♡ *What has been your experience of feeling a part of a "world family?"*

♡ *Have you met strangers that quickly felt like "family" to you? How could you recreate that feeling on a more consistent basis with other people in your life?*

No Walking Away

T.J. Broom embraces the concept of a *world family*, particularly when it involves children in need. A strong passion for helping youth, irrespective of culture, creed or color, was seeded in 2003, while he was on his first mission trip to work with orphans in Honduras, and he soon realized that this was his calling.

T.J. and his wife, Kellie, raised three daughters, whom they adopted from Eastern Europe at ages two, seven, and thirteen, helping them to transition from orphanages and abandonment to a loving home. Now that the girls are in their teens and twenties, T.J. has more time to spend on projects that he feels guided to do.

On his days off from his responsibilities as the battalion chief of his city's fire department, T.J. can often be found volunteering to help others, especially children. He says, "I used to work several jobs to earn extra money, but now I find it feels better to do things for free. It's far more fulfilling."

On a recent mission trip to Motastepe, Nicaragua, a village of overwhelming poverty, T.J. and thirty-two members of his church's youth group completed major repairs to a local church, and with supplies that they had brought with them, set up a "store" where people could pick up clothes, shoes, toys, or whatever they needed for free.

As T.J. was standing near a bus, out of the corner of his eye he noticed a woman waving to him, trying to get his attention. "I walked toward her, and I saw that she was pointing to a tiny girl with a huge hole in her throat. The hole, red and raw around the edges, was protected by a metal plate held in place by a leather string tied around her neck.

Through a translator, T.J. learned that little Emely's upper trachea began to close when she was just an infant. The Nicaraguan doctors created an alternative airway by opening up her throat and putting a metal plate with a hole in it over the opening to keep foreign objects out.

As T.J. looked into the large, deep brown eyes of this five-year-old and saw the expression of concern on her mother's face, he knew that he couldn't walk away. "There was this vulnerable, open and trusting little face, a foot away from me," said T.J. "I felt that God was saying, 'See this. Fix this. I know you can't fix it directly, but you can find someone who can.' I felt like I had no choice. I told Emely's mom, Sanchez, that I would see what I could do."

Those words might be casually tossed out by people wanting to walk away and not get involved, but not by T.J. What he had seen had left an unforgettable impression on him. There was no turning back on his promise.

The next sixteen months proved to be nothing short of a miracle. Back in the United States, T.J. was able to raise $8,000, and locate an ear, nose, and throat specialist, who, upon seeing the photo of Emely's throat, agreed to operate on her for free. Then there were the miles of red tape and paper work necessary to bring her and her mom to Florida for a few months for the surgery and recovery period.

T.J., who has gotten to spend more time with Emely, says, "She is spunky and a regular jokester." She treats T.J. like a dad as she climbs up on his lap to hug him. She tells him, "I want to be pretty from the neck down," but her mother's tears express the reality of her daughter's fragile health and concern about the difficult surgery.

In fact, after the initial surgery in late 2009, when Emely had returned to Nicaragua, there were complications. She got pneumonia and subsequently went into respiratory arrest. T.J., as concerned as though she were his own child, anxiously waited while the doctors and Emely fought for her life. Once stabilized, she came back to Florida with her mom for another two-and-a-half months.

During this time, T.J. and other members of his church, as well as the local community, came together to support this little dynamo and her devoted mom. One church member was dedicated to their care throughout their stay in Florida. Others contributed their time, money, homes, and affection. A philanthropic couple who happened to hear about Emely's precarious situation, had a new home built in Nicaragua for Emely and her family, so that when she returned, she could live in a healthier environment.

Although at this point, the doctors have decided that the safest and best plan is to wait for another year to do the next necessary surgery, T.J. is prepared to do whatever it takes to give Emely the best chance that he can for a long and healthy life.

♡ *Have you ever had a desire to help people living in another part of the world?*

♡ *How does it touch you to see people living in poverty, knowing that there are few options for change?*

♡ *What would you do if you had increased or unlimited resources of time or money?*

Host Dad

For several years, Duane Daily, a high school speech teacher from Manhattan, Kansas, would spend a week or two each summer at his family's Colorado mountain cabin. Each time, he would be accompanied by an international student from countries such as France, Germany, Switzerland, and Brazil. The changing faces and charming accents of these boys became a part of the summertime ritual for neighbors, while the teens were happy to experience the cooler weather of the Rocky Mountains.

Duane was a *host dad* through American Field Service, the world's largest community-based volunteer organization, "dedicated to building a more just and peaceful world through international student exchange."

When he had first heard about the program, it had reminded Duane of a life-altering experience that he had had when he was twenty-three years old. Through a 4-H program, he had lived in Egypt with three different host families for six-and-a-half months. "It was such an incredible opportunity to get out in the world and to participate in the lives of people of a vastly different culture," he said. "It also gave me a perspective of what foreigners must go through when they come to the United States."

Because of his experience, Duane decided to open his home to exchange students as a way to broaden their understanding of Americans and their way of life. Each student that he hosted meant an eleven-month commitment, from August through June, with full responsibility for all of their food and lodging, as well as their safety and well-being.

"It was a challenge because every kid was different, but no matter what country they were from, the behavior of teenagers is the same," he said. "It was especially tough when they left. It felt like the empty-nest syndrome every year. There were tears shed on both sides."

The greatest joy for Duane has been in developing and maintaining ongoing relationships with those whom he considers family. "I have two German granddaughters," he says with pride, referring to the children of his first host student, Daniel, whom he recently visited. To the girls, he is "Grandpa."

Altogether Duane has hosted six international students. He loved watching each of the students grow and expand their perspective about themselves and about their host country. For some, it was a major transformation.

Felix, for example, had a "bit of an attitude" when he arrived from France, where he said that Americans have a strong and relatively negative reputation. However, by the end of the eleven months, Felix wrote a letter to the editor, summing up his experience:

Folks not convinced of the greatness of Kansas should spend time here. Coming from a large city in France, I must say that I was slightly afraid when I heard that I would live in the middle of Kansas for a year. I spent the beginning of the summer explaining to my family that it was really Manhattan, Kansas —that it had nothing to do with New York ... and getting disappointed reactions or bad jokes about cowboys and buffaloes. I had opportunities to learn about the rich historical, geographic and cultural heritage of the region and to visit museums and expositions ... I had a colorful and rich stay ... The person that I want to thank the most is Duane Daily for hosting me during this whole year, for having the patience to take care of me and help me in my everyday life in the United States ... He made it an extraordinary life experience that I will never forget. Thank you for everything.

♡ *Have you ever thought about adopting or helping to parent someone else's child?*

♡ *Would you consider being a host parent to a foreign student for a few months or a year?*

♡ *In what ways could you share your knowledge and love with the children that are in your life currently?*

A Little Bit Goes a Long Way

"Are you going to take a vacation this summer?" I ask Tammy, a lovely young Vietnamese-American woman, who is giving me a manicure in her mom's nail salon.

She pauses, smiles, and replies: "No, I am going to work very hard and save money."

Tammy routinely works about ten hours a day six days a week.

She politely answers my questions, sharing part of her personal story, as she continues filing. I learn that Tammy moved to the United States ten years ago with her mother and sister, where they became citizens. She is twenty-seven now.

"It's so difficult for many of my cousins and family still living in Vietnam," says Tammy. "I try to help them whenever I can. It's easy for me not to buy something that I want or not to go out for an expensive meal because I know that others have so little, and the little bit that I can give goes such a long way."

Tammy explains that in the village where she used to live, there are still people, many of them elderly, who are sleeping on dirt. "Their homes are nothing more than a tent with old sticks as poles and some leaves on the top. When I was growing up, we did not have much, but my family was more fortunate—we had a house and wooden beds to sleep on."

Her family has a tradition that they have been practicing for many years. "On our New Year, we give help to poor farm families who have little to survive on." Tammy was glad to be able to send about $700 that year —enough to buy a month's supply of rice, as well as basic things such as salt and sugar, that can feed about fifteen to twenty families.

Two years ago, Tammy went to Vietnam with her sister and boyfriend to personally hand out the rice. "The people were so grateful and happy, and it made us feel good. It doesn't seem like a lot to us, but it means a great deal to people who have nothing. While we were there, we felt guilty spending money on ourselves when there was so much poverty around us. I couldn't think about spending even $10 on a massage when I knew that my cousins were working all day in the hot sun for about $1.50 a day."

Tammy's father still lives in Vietnam. He has a farm, and tries to earn extra money by giving people rides on his scooter. It has become dangerous going into big cities, where traffic is so bad. Last month, he took someone into the city, a three-hour trip by scooter each way, and he received only $10. Tammy was so mad when she learned that he was given so little. She says, "It's easy for me to make an extra $10 or more. I now send him money every month so that he can stop driving people into the cities and stay in the village where it is safer."

When I commented on how wonderful it is that she is so

generous and helpful to her family and others, she replies: "It's nothing compared to what other people do. I could do so much more. But I am still young and have many more years to give."

♡ *Do you have family or friends living in another country who are in need?*

♡ *If so, how are you able to be supportive to them?*

♡ *What kind of a response would you hope to have from them if you required assistance?*

Creating Community

Never doubt that a small group of thoughtful committed citizens can change the world, indeed, it's the only thing that ever has.

– Margaret Mead

From the time I was seven years old, our family life revolved around Art's Variety Store. I was excited when my dad purchased the store, which sold candy, chips, and comic books, but what I discovered in later years was the value that it offered to the community. It was a comfortable "third place" to go between home and work. It became a daily ritual for many customers, including cops, truck drivers, postal carriers, construction workers, and retirees, who would stop in at "Art's" for coffee, conversation, and connection—a tradition that my dad and family members kept going for almost fifty-two years. My dad finally retired at 83, but Art's Variety Store continues to be a friendly gathering place.

Trends indicate that we are reclaiming a deeper appreciation for old-time values that has been missing for decades, accompanied by feelings of contentment and well-being that come from being a part of a community. No matter how we characterize a community—living in a neighborhood, being part of a social, religious, or ethnic group—our common connection creates a sense of belonging, and offers a way to take care of each other's needs.

While churches and spiritual centers have traditionally offered opportunities for coming together to support each other, today there are more casual communities being formed on the Internet via social networking sites, as well as through more typical person-to-person, physical and social connections.

If anything, these tough economic times have shown us that perhaps nothing will be as important for our welfare and survival as creating and living in community. It may be necessary to take on the responsibility for not only our own and our family's well-being, but that of our neighbors, and those who can't take care of themselves. Our physical, emotional, and financial health may depend on how we share our food, home, resources, and skills.

Communities give people opportunities to contribute and collaborate. Big or small, there are innumerable ways to help. Whether it's their time, money, vote, or actions, most people are grateful to be a part of something that is bringing about positive change for individuals, their community, country, or planet.

A Call to Service

I'm always astonished by what one caring, focused individual, or a small group of dedicated people, can do to inspire a community to action. Sometimes all it takes to get people involved is to come up with a good idea, find a way to get the word out, and make it easy to participate.

When President-elect Barack Obama put out a call for people to dedicate January 19, 2009, as a "National Day of Service," Rachelle Zola heeded that call.

With a ready laugh and a positive attitude that makes her fun to be around, Rachelle joined a group whose goal was to collect clothing and school supplies for students in four of the community's neediest schools, as well as food to replenish the well-used local food bank.

Although she had just moved to a new neighborhood, and had met only four of her neighbors, Rachelle targeted the 251 homes in her homeowners' association to request donations. She didn't have high expectations; she was aware that many people might be too busy to even read the fliers that she planned to distribute. But that didn't stop her.

With the assistance of her 13-year-old neighbor, Matt, she placed bright yellow and orange fliers throughout the neighborhood. "We made it specific and easy to participate," said Rachelle. "All people had to do was to leave donations on their front porches to be picked up on January 19th."

Rachelle and Wendy, a neighbor who volunteered her truck and her time, started out at ten o'clock that morning to pick up donations in each of the fourteen cul de sacs. What they found was beyond their wildest dreams. "We were blown away! It felt like Christmas, when Santa came and gave you everything that you wanted and so much more," Rachelle said. The porches were filled with food and supplies, and each time they turned a corner, they saw the same vision of abundance.

"Wow! Look at all this stuff! Can you believe it?" they said, looking at each other in amazement.

"It was over the top!" said Rachelle. In one week, with 48 percent of the neighborhood participating, the group collected three overflowing truckloads of food, clothing, and supplies.

But the rewards went beyond the donated items. Rachelle was astounded by the number of handwritten thank-you notes left with the donations, as well as the number of people who personally came out to express their appreciation for giving them an opportunity to get involved in the project. Their efforts had inspired a currency of generosity, goodwill, and gratitude in their neighborhood and beyond

"Many times people are just waiting to be asked to help because they don't know what they can do to make a difference," says Rachelle. "I feel so blessed to be a part of a community that really wants to show up."

Acts of Urban Kindness

The Washington, D.C. Metro area is known for many things, but openness and friendliness probably aren't prominent on that list. That changed, however, when a major blizzard stopped the city in its governmental tracks, causing numerous people to rely on each other for such basic needs as food, shelter, warmth, and electricity.

In February 2010, the city was hit by two major snow storms back to back. It was the biggest snowfall that D.C. had experienced in sixty years, with more than forty inches of snow immobilizing many sections of the city. Hundreds of homes were without power for three to five days. Even the mail service was disrupted for two weeks. There were no hotel rooms available, even if you could drive to one outside of the blackout area, which most people couldn't do.

Joanne, a D.C. Metro resident for thirty years, was pleasantly surprised by how neighbors and strangers alike helped each other during the storms. "A crisis seems to bring out the best in people," she said. Her neighborhood e-mail *listserv* proved to be a quick and effective way to ask for help or to respond to the needs of others.

One woman, whose home had gas heat, extended an invitation to anyone in the neighborhood without power to come and stay or to warm up and take a hot shower. This woman also offered the use of her extra two bedrooms and a bathroom to anyone, including complete strangers, in need of a place to stay.

Many who had power gave those who were without an opportunity to charge their cell phone or other electronic devices. "That's not something that happens on a typical day in D.C., where high-powered attorneys, doctors, and professionals live busy, private lives," said Joanne.

But it wasn't the first time she had witnessed such generosity in response to a *listserv* request. Just prior to the storms, one woman, who volunteered at a Kitchen that fed breakfast and dinner to 300 needy people daily, put in a request through her *listserv* asking for help to replenish the extremely low supplies of cereal and coffee. When Joanne drove to this woman's house to bring her donations, she was astounded to see the entire porch piled high with cans of coffee and boxes of cereal that neighbors had dropped off.

"I have never experienced this kind of reaching out and selflessness," says Joanne. "When there's a unified, common dilemma, a shared strife, it forces people to come together and seek each other's assistance. They find out that people aren't so cold and distant after all."

♡ *Have you ever organized or been a part of a community project?*

♡ *What were you able to accomplish collectively that you couldn't have done on your own?*

♡ *Did it enhance your sense of belonging to the community as you worked cooperatively together?*

♡ *Did that experience give you a different perspective about your own life situation?*

"It Takes a Village . . ."

Whether to raise a child, to care for an elder, to help someone with an illness, or to support those who've had a personal loss or suffered a financial setback, it's a comfort to know that we don't have to do it alone. One of the benefits of living in a *village* is the communal sharing that takes the overwhelming burden off of any one individual.

This is what can happen when a community pools its resources to support its members:

In Arizona, when Sonya's husband Shawn lost his job where he'd worked for seven years, it was a struggle to support their family of six. As the weeks and months passed, all financial focus was put on basics: food, utilities, shelter and transportation. Sonya says, "What we learned during this tough time was that we have the most amazing family, church members, and friends. Here's what they did for us: They hired us, found us work, passed along our resumes, fed us, clothed us, gave us gift cards for gas and groceries, and prayed for us. And when these gifts arrived, including anonymous envelopes filled with cash, it was always perfect timing."

Sonya continues, "Probably the most memorable gift of all was the time I was resting on the couch with my youngest son late one evening. The doorbell rang, but when I opened the door no one was there. Instead, I saw boxes and bags filled with groceries covering our doorstep and spilling out onto the front lawn. Incredible!"

Exactly nine months, to the day, that he was laid off, Shawn got a job offer. Now they can hardly wait to do some of the same things for others who are facing similar struggles. Sonya says, "We've been blessed beyond measure by receiving, and it's definitely made us more inspired to give."

Another example of a community's *currency of love* is illustrated in these excerpts from a Christmas letter that I received from long time friends, Don and Margaret Johnson, who recently celebrated their 40th wedding anniversary:

Dear Friends,

Our year was filled with an over abundance of blessings. You may wonder how we can say this when you read the rest of this year's Christmas letter.

Our year started off normal, with Don working at Trader Joe's and Margaret working in wholesale gift sales in New Mexico and

West Texas, until one day when a retired doctor friend suggested that Margaret didn't look right. We took Margaret to the hospital where they did a series of tests, including an MRI. A doctor, whom we had never met, came in and told Margaret: "I don't know how to say this any other way than to just blurt it out: You have a brain tumor." Our world stopped. Two days later, Margaret underwent a six-hour surgery, during which she had a stroke that affected her left side and speech.

This is where our blessings began. Our church, neighbors, friends, sisters and brothers rallied around us. On the day of the surgery, there were as many as 27 people at one time with Don, praying and giving love and support. Margaret spent a week in ICU and a month in rehab.

Upon her release, members of our church came to us and said: "We have put together a care giver team that is going to be on call 24/7." Don was able to continue his job, while Margaret's "band of Angels," as we called them, hovered over her and took care of all her needs.

Our customers, employers, and strangers have come to our aid in so many ways, including cash donations, homemade cookies and dinners, and monthly pledges of support. [We even received an anonymous cashiers' check for $1500.] Today we had 16 teenagers from our church do a total clean up of our yard, raking and bagging leaves. They then treated us to a pasta dinner and offered prayers for Margaret.

We hope none of you have had to experience the year we have, but just in case, please let us know so we can include you on our prayer list and do what we can to lift you and let you know you are loved.

We love ya bunches,
Don and Margaret

Although Margaret was told by a number of doctors that she had only a year or less to live, she has just achieved that one year mark and is off of chemo for now.

♡ *How do you define a community? What does that look like in your life?*

♡ *Are you part of a community currently? Does it give you hope that you would have support if you needed it or that you would have a way to help others?*

♡ *What kind of a community do you envision as you age?*

Faces of a Local Community: Sarasota, Florida

Community is usually created intentionally rather than by happenstance, the result of one, two, or a small number of individuals who have the desire and vision to bring people together in ordinary and sometimes in extraordinary ways.

There are endless possibilities for forming and being part of a community, as varied as the faces and personalities of its members. It can also take on different attributes depending on location and individuals' needs.

Living in Florida, a state known for its part-time residents, in a Sarasota condo complex, separated from neighbors by stucco walls, I realize that close proximity doesn't guarantee that one is a part of a community. Luckily, retired neighbors, Mike and Martina Venz, love to serve as social connectors for the ninety families who consider this complex home. They host an annual Christmas pool party, enhanced by lighted palms and the live sounds of a steel drum, to provide an opportunity for residents to meet each other and to support a local food bank (through donations of canned goods). They also do landscaping and organize mulching and planting parties to beautify the grounds at little or no cost to condo members. Mike and Martina form the core of this community and foster fellowship for the sheer joy of it.

Pirates Cove is a very different type of intentional community, one that came together out of necessity. According to an article in the Sarasota Herald-Tribune, written by Kim Hackett, there are thousands of homeless people in this region, including families with children. Throughout Southwest Florida, there are hundreds of tent communities, where people without jobs or homes live "in the woods." One of these, Pirates Cove, marked by a skull and crossbones with a sign reading "Do Not Enter … Thank You," is a circle of tents and tarps, well-hidden in Sarasota, where residents share food, blankets, supplies, and humor to help each other survive. Kim's article states, "The dozen or so homeless people who are camped at Pirates Cove have formed a community in which they are more dependent on and care more about their neighbors than in many subdivisions." They cook together, celebrate birthdays and special events, and keep a guest tent set up in case unexpected visitors show up. They even have a "mayor" and their own established set of rules.

The following stories, which all take place in Sarasota, offer a microcosmic view of the variety of community gatherings that provide social connection, support, and a sense of belonging.

Tai Chi on Siesta Beach

Siesta Key Beach has been named the second most beautiful beach in the United States. But its value goes beyond its pristine beauty and the healing qualities of its white quartz crystal sand. What makes Siesta Beach, and all of Sarasota, so special are the people who generously share their unique gifts and talents with friends, neighbors, and visitors alike.

Richard and Diana Daffner, longtime residents of Siesta Key, love sharing their passions, one of which is the practice of tai chi on the beach. Every Monday night anywhere from ten to twenty-five people gather to participate in this centering experience. In unison, their feet in soft, sensuous sand, they do slow meditative movements, as they watch the orange glow of the setting sun casting reflections on the water.

"I love tai chi chih," says Diana. "It's so rewarding to introduce others to this magical movement practice, which, if one is focused, can relieve stress and even change thought patterns."

Diana considers it a gift to herself, as well as to the participants. "When I have a group behind me doing tai chi chih, the energy is palpable as it gets stronger. And I love seeing how much more rested and open everyone is afterward."

What's amazing is that the Daffners have been offering this gift to the community for free for more than fifteen years.

Meditations and Celebrations

As a young girl growing up in Antigua in the West Indies, Jo Mooy knew that she was going to do something big that would have a positive, but subtle, effect on the world. She said, "I always felt guided, protected, and most of all *directed* to who I needed to meet, where I needed to go, and what I needed to do."

That guidance led Jo, as an adult, to move to Sarasota in December of 2005, where she chose to actively participate in and create community. In January 2006, Jo brought together a group of eight women to meditate monthly in each other's homes. Within two years, this Women's Meditation Group expanded to bi-monthly meetings of 50+ women in a permanent setting, where it has become a refuge, a spiritual gathering, and a place of community. Each time the women gather, they share how much the meditation group means to them: "It has become my spiritual home," and "I feel safe, loved, and accepted at these gatherings." This is a "family of women" who care deeply for one another.

Whether on the beach or in a spiritual center, Jo, and her partner Patricia Cockerill create a sacred space for women to meet, to meditate, to learn, and to share. It doesn't matter what your religious beliefs may be or what you do for a living; you are invited to open your heart to others in loving community and service.

January 2011 marked the five year anniversary of this women's meditation group with close to 70 women gathered in a circle. The message was clear: "Honor the women who walk on this path sharing the truth that *there is only love.*" Meetings are free, but generosity overflows as the basket is passed around for "love offerings" to thank the center for the use of the space and to contribute to the "Mayor's Feed the Hungry Program." The group had set a goal of raising $1200 for the needy in 2010. It had seemed like a stretch considering the tough economic times, but the women surpassed that goal and contributed a record $2152!

Jo has won numerous awards for this work that she has carried out so lovingly. Through her online newsletter, *Spiritual Connections*, subscribed to by over 500 women, and her *StarSoundings Journal*, also online, she offers a wonderful resource to the community and reaches out to an even broader global family.

Jo and Patricia's *currency of love* is connection, communication, and community.

They make it easy to participate in creating a better world.

♡ *When do you feel a sense of belonging and most connected to others?*

♡ *What makes it easy for you to participate in a group activity or project?*

♡ *What are your gifts or talents that you would like to share with a community?*

Cooking Up Community

"I've always felt abundant in my life. My measure of wealth is love, and has been since I was a child," says Megaera Putney, who was one of eight children born to missionary parents. They lived in a tiny, three bedroom house with one bathroom. "My family was very affectionate, with lots of hugs and kisses. A day never passed without hearing and saying 'I love you' more than once." Megaera learned that sharing love was the most important thing in life—"far more valuable than money or things."

As an adult, Megaera and her partner had a remodeling business, through which they purchased and sold numerous houses. But like many people, they lost everything in the collapse of the real estate market, including their home.

For some this type of loss is devastating, but Megaera is undaunted. "My home is where I am, not the house that I live in," she says. "The same goes for family—my family is the community of friends I share love with, not just my relatives."

She considers her measure of wealth and greatest asset to be her community. "I know that if we ever have a crisis, either environmental or economic, we could rely on each other to get through it. My version of planning for an emergency is stocking my pantry with food that could feed a lot of people. My concern isn't what *I* would need, but what *we* would need."

One of the ways Megaera expresses love is through her cooking. Her Thanksgiving dinners are shared with 40 to 50 friends. She prepares homemade meals for co-workers, and bakes exquisite cakes to celebrate friends' birthdays. She loves to create communal gatherings. Not surprisingly, everyone wants to be on "Megaera's list," which continues to expand with the inclusion of *friends of friends* and newcomers.

When asked what draws 50+ people to respond to a last minute email about a party at someone's home or at a local restaurant, she says, "I think on the surface people come for fun, for food, music and dancing, but underneath they come for love and affection. When we hug and kiss, we are really acknowledging each other at a heart level. We get filled up with love."

Don, one of Megaera's fans, refers to her as "our den mother." Others describe being enveloped in her warm embrace as being welcomed by the "goddess of love."

Megaera herself admits, "It's really quite selfish. I do it for me. I get fed by it. Whenever I invite people, I know that I will get 50 hugs and kisses when I come in and 50 when I leave!"

♡ *How do you define wealth?*

♡ *In what ways do you consider yourself wealthy?*

♡ *How do you share your gifts, talents, and wealth with others?*

Three
Gifts of the Heart

It is only with the heart that one can see rightly;
what is essential is invisible to the eye.
— Antoine de Saint Exupery, *The Little Prince*

When we consider what positively impacts our life, it's usually the gifts of the heart—expressions of love, intimacy, compassion, trust, empathy, and inclusion—that matter most. The people in our lives who see and listen to us, who accept us for who we are, without trying to change us, make us feel special and valued.

We all have a need for love, affection, respect, and connection. That doesn't change much throughout our life. As we attempt to dispel the feeling that we are separate, we realize that there's no greater gift that we can give each other than the gift of our presence.

Rachelle knows this. Whenever she meets someone, no matter their outer appearance, she thinks, "*You're easy to love.*" She's quick to listen for the voices within each person: what she calls the "first voice" —which often drives people away with words and actions that are unloveable —and the "second voice," which is saying, "Don't listen to the first voice; I *am* loveable."

Rachelle believes that we all do crazy things out of fear. "I have to believe that what I perceive is not the whole story. I know that I am loved and loveable, and that other people are too. Underneath, we are all the same." Rachelle sees everyone as magnificent, and invites each person not only to receive love, but to own it.

In the end, it isn't the material things that bring us happiness and comfort, but the friends and loved ones by our side. Among our treasures are the memories of those we've loved, the laughter and joy experienced with friends, family, and even strangers, and the ways that we've enriched the lives of others in our giving and receiving that add value and meaning to our lives.

Remember the story in the introduction about my grandfather's silver dollars? For me, it's not those silver dollars from my childhood that I want to hold, but the care-worn hands of the grandfather who gave them to me. And I realize that it's up to me to use my own hands and heart to create precious experiences and memories for others.

Intangible Expressions of Love

Too often we underestimate the power of a touch, a smile,
a kind word, a listening ear, an honest compliment,
or the smallest act of caring, all of which
have the potential to turn a life around.

– Leo Buscaglia

We don't need money to contribute to the well-being of others. Intangible gifts of the heart—laughter, joy, gratitude, kindness, or simply withholding negative thoughts and judgments —can be a *currency of love* that offers immeasurable service.

For instance, have you ever considered that restraining yourself from complaining can be an expression of love, a gift to those around you? More than six million people believe so and have purchased Complaint Free bracelets through the non-profit organization, *A Complaint Free World*, headed by Pastor Will Bowen of Kansas City, Missouri. The idea is to wear the purple bracelet on one wrist and switch it to the other wrist any time you complain. If you can make it for twenty-one days in a row without switching, then you are on your way to maintaining a positive attitude that anyone around you will appreciate. Despite a world that offers innumerable reasons to express our negative comments, millions are finding that there are just as many positives to celebrate.

Deep listening is another valuable gift that we can give to each other—listening with undivided attention not only with our ears, but more importantly with our hearts. I was reminded of this a couple of weeks ago, when I was in a rush to head home from a class, and someone, whom I'd just met, asked if I had a few minutes to hear a story she wanted to share. My mind immediately jumped in with *I'm so busy. I have so much to do. I can't take the time right now.* Fortunately, I was able to stop the inner chatter. I realized there was nothing more important in that moment than to sit and to listen to this woman. I'm grateful that I did. Her inspiring story moved me to tears, as did the telling of it for her. And the memory of that exchange continues to remind me to stop and listen.

Intangible gifts are free and have an enduring value. Following are other examples of intangible expressions of love, which cause me to consider how I can give more of myself, which has nothing to do with the dollars in my pocket.

Laughter Heals

We don't laugh because we're happy—we're happy because we laugh.
– Dr. Madan Kataria

You would have to be comatose to not laugh when you're around Taulere Appel. At a party several months ago, I had the pleasure of meeting with Taulere and her husband Arrone and laughing with them for the entire time that we were in conversation. It felt great—like a mini-vacation from my much-too-serious self.

Three years ago, Taulere discovered Laughter Yoga, which was developed in India in 1995 by Dr. Madan and Madhari Kataria. Taulere is now devoted to this daily practice which has changed her life: "I'm not as stressed, I have much less ego, enjoy better quality of relationships, and I've not been sick once in three years." She continues, "I've found one of the best things to be the joy and freedom to be more of who I am, to share happiness and love freely, and to laugh as hard and as often as I want, without people thinking I'm crazy."

Another amazing benefit of laughter is improved memory. Taulere and Arrone recently visited Arrone's 93-year-old mom who has dementia. Before making the 2,000-mile trip, they decided they were going to be happy no matter what. It worked. The entire visit was filled with laughter. They noticed that Arrone's mom was more coherent and communicative. In fact, in a moment of clarity, she said, "Laugher's good for everyone. Being happy is a much better way to be in the world."

And Taulere couldn't agree more. She shared an interesting statistic: Adults laugh about fourteen times a day, but that was cut by half after September 11. People were more stressed and serious. We both agreed: We don't need a survey to tell us that the decrease in laughter has continued well into these challenging economic times.

Taulere laughs for at least an hour every day. She believes laughter is an act of kindness that can easily be shared. "Happiness is as contagious as fear. We can choose what we want to be spreading in the world." She freely shares her gift with others by hosting weekly Laughter Yoga sessions in her home.

My curiosity was piqued, and I decided to attend a session and to experience an evening of laughter. It was a bit daunting to walk into a roomful of people I didn't know, and I wondered if I'd be able to comfortably participate. No problem. Taulere led all six of us through a series of exercises that had us all laughing for a solid hour. That was a record for me. At the end, I felt so much lighter, and I realized as we hugged good-bye that there really are no strangers.

For a year, Taulere hosted twenty-minute phone laughter sessions. While she no longer does this regularly, she still volunteers as needed. She's currently working on a project to bring laughter to schools as a way to promote wellness and world peace.

Laugher is a natural part of her persona and when things in life go haywire, as they sometimes will, Taulere is able to just laugh it off.

♡ *How often do you laugh? How does it make you feel?*

♡ *Have others been caught up in your laughter?*

♡ *What is the funniest thing that has ever happened to you?*

♡ *Can you share that story with someone today.*

"Attitude of Gratitude"

> *Feeling gratitude and not expressing it is like*
> *wrapping a present and not giving it.*
> – William Arthur Ward

Over six years ago, I started a daily gratitude journal. First thing each morning, I write three things for which I am grateful. I now have several books filled with proof that my life is, indeed, abundant. One lesson that I've learned is that the more I've focused on and expressed the blessings in my life, the more reasons I have to be thankful.

While I may not always be happy about everything that happens in my life, I've discovered that eventually even those events often turn out to be beneficial. A grateful attitude helps me to get to that place more quickly.

While most of my journal entries are about family, friends,

and health, I also express appreciation for the lessons that I'm learning (even the difficult ones), as well as for the acts of kindness that I witness or experience daily.

I've noticed that there are few entries about money, although I am grateful when wealth in any form flows into my life. Over time I've noticed a change in the way I feel about money. While in the past, I'd mentally grumble over the many checks that I had to write to cover my expenses, I now am thankful that I have the money with which to pay them. And I'm even taking it a step further by sending blessings to whoever receives this paper currency.

I have a picture of gratitude that helps me put things in perspective whenever I'm in a funky mood:

Several years ago, Sara, my friend of over twenty years, had just finished a round of chemo treatments. I had brought lunch to her home and spent an afternoon sitting with her. Being there brought up memories of the numerous Thanksgivings celebrated in Sara and her husband Bill's mountain home. We would all gather around the table and share what we were grateful for, before joining in a resounding and sustained "yum yum yum…" as we prepared to eat the meal.

Now, as I looked at Sara, reclining on the couch—bald, beautiful and beaming with a light that I couldn't imagine being taken away —she said to me, "I'm a lucky duck! I have so much to be thankful for. I'm happy to be here." She recounted all of the people for whom she was grateful: her husband, two daughters, and her many friends…

I thought, *Wow! How can I live with such appreciation? What a gift Sara is in my life.*

The next day, she called and left a message to express how grateful she was for our time together and for the foot massage I'd given to her.

Thankfully, I still have that recording of her voice. Sara departed several days later.

♡ *What do you consider a blessing now that you didn't perceive that way initially?*

♡ *What are you most grateful for in your life? Write it down.*

♡ *How could you make expressions of gratitude a daily practice?*

Measure of Happiness

Success is not the key to happiness. Happiness is the key to success.
If you love what you are doing, you will be successful.
– Albert Schweitzer

If you knew that your happiness could positively affect not only your friends and those around you, but their friends ... and even friends of friends ... would you not want to be contagious for a good cause?

In December 2008, the findings of a happiness study conducted by Harvard Medical School's Professor Christakis, and James Fowler of the University of California in San Diego, stated that when individuals are happy it triggers a chain reaction that can affect others up to three degrees, and last for up to a year. Their study of 5000 individuals over 20 years revealed that "happiness spreads through social networks like an emotional contagion." Fowler commented: "Having $5000 extra increased a person's chances of being happy by about 2%," but he went on to say that someone that you don't even know [ie. a friend of a friend] "could have a greater influence [on your happiness] than hundreds of dollars in your pocket."

In the Himalayan country of Bhutan, with its predominantly Buddhist culture, the focus of its public policies is the GNH— *Gross National Happiness* quotient. King Jigme Singye Wangchuk, who coined the term in 1972, believed "Gross National Happiness is more important that Gross National Product." It was later supported by his son, who took over the throne in 2006. The Fifth King of Bhutan states: "Our most important goal is the peace and happiness of our people."

Gail Gordon, a friend of mine who recently visited Bhutan, says, "I felt as though I were experiencing a true life *Camelot*." She found the residents, most of them living off the land, to be friendly and happy. She would often see signs on cars that read, "I love my king." Gail says, "There is no crime in Bhutan where citizens have a respect for nature, the cycle of life, and their fellow man."

According to Wikepedia, this Buddhist culture considers the key components of happiness to be: "physical, mental and spiritual health, time-balance, community and cultural vitality, education, living standards, good governance and ecological vitality."

Surveys of a segment of the population are done twice yearly to ensure that these values are afforded Bhutan's 600,000 citizens.

In contrast, in the United States, the *pursuit of happiness* is stated as one of our inalienable rights in the Declaration of Independence, yet I can't remember the last time that it was an expressed consideration in developing our government policies. We might ask: how can we as individuals, and as a nation, incorporate happiness as a key measure of our wealth and welfare? Perhaps when elected officials can put aside their individual differences and political agendas to support the well-being of its citizens, the pursuit of happiness will feel like a more attainable goal.

I spoke about this concept with David Rubin, a successful businessman, who brings that philosophy to his company, where he talks to his employees, asking if they are taking the time to pursue what brings them joy, whether it's tennis, painting, or being with their family … and then he suggests that it be part of their job description. His reasoning is simple: "If we don't take the time to do the things we love and be with the people we love, what are we living for?"

David also shares, "Whenever I play golf, I consider the winner of the game to be the one who has the most fun."

"Using happiness as our yardstick, how are we enjoying and winning at the game of life?" asks David.

♡ *When were you the happiest in your life? Can you recapture the essence of that experience?*

♡ *What makes you happy now? When you are feeling happy, how can you share it with more people?*

♡ *How can you incorporate happiness into your businesses, as well as your personal life?*

The Gift of Presence

It's not what you look at that matters,
it's what you see.

— Henry David Thoreau

There are many in our society who feel invisible. This can be especially true of street people, the elderly, and the mentally or physically handicapped. We walk by them either not seeing them or avoiding their gaze because it's uncomfortable. Oftentimes, those who feel invisible have an even greater need for a loving touch, a kind word, or a look that says, "I truly see you!"

Perhaps there are times when you, too, are not being seen or heard. It makes you feel irrelevant as though who you are and what you have to offer is insignificant. While most of us have someone who acknowledges our presence and supports our sense of self-worth, that's not the reality for everyone.

This is evidenced in the following story about events involving a local street person, which I witnessed and was a part of. However, with no subsequent opportunity to talk with this man, I chose to write from his perspective to maintain anonymity, as well as to convey emotions I could only imagine.

61

"Hey! There's *somebody* in here!"

I don't mean to yell at them. I'm so angry after leaning against a tree for more than an hour at a bustling Saturday market, with a sign and a metal cup held out, with not a single person looking at me or offering a coin as they scurry past with downcast eyes. "You don't give a damn!" I shout as they make a wider path around me.

What are they afraid of? That I might hurt them? That they might catch something? That I might ask for more than they want to give? Do they not want to be confronted with someone who's ugly in their beautiful world? Or perhaps they just don't want their happy day disrupted with the reality that not all is well in the world.

Some suggest that I'm a fraud, and I want to ask, "Would you trade places with me?"

All around me people are smiling, talking with friends, walking arm-in-arm with loved ones, totally caught up in their own lives. It's not that they're mean-spirited, but most people are simply unconscious of what they don't want to see or acknowledge.

I feel like I don't exist. Don't they know that there's a real person inside of this decrepit, scarred face and body?

It's humiliating to have to ask for anything from strangers, and when they do give me money, they usually don't look at me, as though they've fulfilled their obligation to give to the less fortunate and don't want any further engagement.

I often spend time in places that draw a lot of people, not only because there's a greater chance that more kind-hearted people will drop something in my cup, but because I want to be a part of a group, to talk to someone who cares about how I am, and asks about what's important in my life, or who simply sees and acknowledges me. Is that really so much to ask?

A few months ago, I was at the edge of a crowd of people who were listening to music on a hot summer night. A beautiful woman with a big smile walked up to me. I was expecting her to drop some coins in my cup and walk away, but instead she came closer to see me, face to face, and asked me how I was doing. I was touched that Shell—that was her name—not only came right up to me, but spent time asking me about myself. As I shared my story about how I got to this place in my life, I was grateful to look into the eyes of someone who truly saw me and didn't turn away. I felt cared about. After Shell left, the friend she was with came to me, placed some coins in my cup, and looked directly at me.

Six months of cold weather passed, and one warm, sunny day, as I sat on a mall bench with my "God Bless You" sign, two women approached without hesitation. One dropped some money into my cup, but I barely noticed because the other had come close to me, looked into my eyes, and quietly asked if I would pray for her. I wondered if the request was sincere, but her kind eyes told me she was a person who saw and appreciated beauty in others.

I asked her what her name was, and she said, "Kimberly."

"Yes, I will pray for you, Kimberly."

She then asked what my name was. "Andrew," I replied.

"And I will pray for you, Andrew," she said, before turning to walk away.

I felt like a different person. I didn't even mind that people kept going past, oblivious. I believed that I, too, had something of value to give, and I fully intended to say a prayer for Kimberly.

I've come to realize that what means the most to me is not the money I collect, but the kind words, the gentle touch, the friendly greeting—the acknowledgment that I'm real. I have feelings. There's a person inside this ugly body.

All I ask is to be seen.

♡ *Have you ever felt invisible? How did that make you feel?*

♡ *What is your reaction when you encounter a street person asking for change?*

♡ *Are you able to let go of the story that you tell yourself about that person, and just see a human being in need?*

♡ *What are you able to give or express that will create a loving experience for both of you?*

Savoring Life

Few people give their full presence with such compassion and openness as David Goliath Ward. A former brother in the Jesuit order for twenty-two years, David has been volunteering in homeless shelters for the last ten years. In his words, he offers his insights about those whom society deems "homeless":

Every day, I witness people who are *houseless*, not homeless. I recently read about a couple who lived in a multimillion-dollar home in the Midwest, who lost everything in the recent market decline, and tragically ended up committing suicide. Now, that's what I call being *homeless*. For me, not having a relationship with God, with others, with the Earth, and not being able to savor life—to be nourished, to feel loved, to experience gratitude—create a sense of homelessness and hopelessness.

Several years ago, I made a wonderful connection with Guillermo, a man from South America, who made his way throughout the United States by hopping trains. With his green card, Guillermo was able to support himself as a roofer when the need arose, until he felt called to move on. A few years later, while on a train headed west, Guillermo accidentally fell off the train, and both his arms were severed below the elbow. When I last saw him, he was being fitted for prostheses and learning how to pick up a ball by shrugging his shoulders.

While life is full of risks, the poor are especially vulnerable because of their lack of financial resources, and oftentimes, all they have is their faith to help them make it through. Guillermo had that faith. The "wealthy" couple committed suicide; Guillermo did not. Although I don't know where he is, Guillermo's richness still touches and inspires me today because he chose to continue, to appreciate the gift of life that he was given.

I've had a longtime love affair with "Christ's poor," even after I left the Jesuit order. After completing massage school, I started giving foot massages at a local homeless shelter. I discovered an amazing synchronicity: The beginning of this mission occurred on

Holy Thursday, the day, according to the Bible, that Christ washed the feet of his disciples. With other massage students, as well as therapists, we felt honored to serve by giving thousands of massages to the homeless for almost seven years.

Life has an interesting way of coming full circle. My own father was once houseless. In time, he was able to create a successful business building homes, which continued for fifty-three years. Although he has transitioned, his legacy, in the form of a trust, has given me the opportunity to help those who find themselves without a place to live.

Through this trust, I've been able to share my abundance, giving more than $100,000 to those in need during a two-year time span. I've felt enriched by my ability to give, and only wish that I had more to offer because the need is so great.

The number of people who are unable to maintain a home continues to grow exponentially, many of whom find themselves *houseless* for the very first time. What is especially upsetting is that many are single women with children. I find the saddest cases to be those who are glazed over and numb. When they are houseless, they can feel uninhabited and vacant.

I've met people from all walks of life at these shelters, who want nothing more than to be productive but can't find jobs. Together we've created gardens with donated land, enabling them to contribute and to be an integral part of a growing and cohesive community. It offers hope.

What I've learned is that people are hungry, not because they don't have food, but because they can't savor life. If you believe that your life is full of lack, then that's all that you can give—lack. It's the marginalized who teach us what life is all about. When you have the vantage point of being at the bottom, that vulnerability takes you to a deeper level of awareness and appreciation. I believe that people can make a difference by living in gratitude.

Most recently, I'm choosing to give in a different, more engaged way. When asked for money for bus fare, I offer to drive the person where they're going; when asked for money for a meal, I personally invite them to a restaurant and sit and eat with them. I've come to realize that if you give of yourself, others will receive what they truly need—presence and friendship.

One afternoon, as I was walking into the bank with a new briefcase, I said hello to three street people sitting on the grass. When I came out minutes later, one of them said, "I sure like that briefcase." I knelt down on the grass, emptied it, and handed the briefcase to him, saying, "Here. It's yours."

The good news and the truth that I've come to realize, is that we are all rich. When someone connects with us on a deep level and we feel loved, then we are rich. Poverty doesn't diminish the richness. It's not about what people have or don't have; it's about what goes on inside us that truly matters. Money doesn't make the world work. It's our ability to give, to share, to love, and to savor life that gives meaning to our existence.

♡ *What helps you to savor life during tough times? How can you help others to do that?*

♡ *What are the things that make you feel connected and give you a feeling of worth?*

♡ *How can you engage more authentically with your friends and family?*

♡ *How can you help others by giving what they really need as opposed to what you have a surplus of?*

Loving Touch

> *Maybe that's why I want to touch people so often—*
> *it's only another way of talking.*
>
> – Georgia O'Keefe

Like most human beings, I thrive on physical touch, both giving and receiving it. It's an expression of caring that needs no words and is one of my favorite ways to convey feelings of love and affection.

There have been studies confirming that babies who are not touched in the early days of their lives have less of a chance of survival than those who receive affection. Fortunately, most people can hardly wait to hold a newborn.

But there are few in our society more in need of physical touch and connection than those at the other end of life. Many in nursing facilities sit and wait for visitors, oftentimes in vain, as people's busy schedules take priority. Other studies have shown that touch is an important element in helping people with dementia to feel better.

If we are fortunate to still have our parents, it can be difficult seeing them as vulnerable and fragile. It's hard to face the fact that it may not be long before we'll be dealing with our own declining bodies. We might consider: How can we gracefully embrace the latter part of our life as we have its other stages? How can we be more loving towards those at the end of their life cycle?

I used to cherish the time spent in the nursing home with my 94-year-old friend Jack. His four-foot-wide smile was as big as he was. He lit up when he saw me, although there were many women for whom he did that. Jack would always tell his daughter, my friend Adie, about those visits: "Linda rubs my back." I smile when I think about those special times that we can no longer share since Jack passed away. He always had a good word for everyone, and each person left him feeling better than when they arrived. At Jack's funeral, Rabbi Glickman beautifully expressed: "Jack didn't have a lot of shekels, but yet he was a very rich man."

Juanita, a woman whom I met at the Colorado "Dances of Universal Peace," has found a wonderful way to bring joy to the lives of nursing-home residents. For many years, she has organized and hosted monthly Elder Dances in Boulder and Denver.

Not sure what to expect, I joined several volunteers to participate in an Elder Dance at a local nursing facility. We gathered in the center of a circle, created by the wheelchair-bound residents, and played music and sang phrases which honored different religions of the world. To "dance" with each of the residents meant holding their hands, gazing into their eyes, and lovingly embracing them as we moved from one to the other.

At first, I was overwhelmed by sadness to see the fragile men and women, many of whom were barely able to walk, speak, or move their bodies. I wondered, *Is this making a difference to them?* I then released the question as I gave my full attention to each one, connecting through eye contact and a loving touch.

I no longer focused on the sagging skin and the drooping mouth, or strained to hear the mumbled words. I saw the joy that each one was able to express through the smile in their eyes or on their lips, through the squeeze of my hand, or in the way they moved their body, as best as they could, to the rhythms of the guitar and drum.

I could see the young man or woman they had once been —someone who used to love to dance. While they now dance inside their memories, I was gifted with a glimpse into their world. I was grateful for this exchange of hearts. We were all seen, touched, and heard, and it was beautiful.

♡ *How do you express caring for the elderly people in your family, neighborhood, or community?*

♡ *How often do you call or send a card to older family members or friends who live a distance from you?*

♡ *The next time you see an elderly neighbor can you take a moment to chat or to listen?*

Compassion

To err is human, to forgive is divine.

– Alexander Pope

We all make mistakes; we all do or say things that we wish we hadn't. When we hurt others, we usually suffer the consequences, whether we're conscious of it or not. And the most difficult person to forgive is often ourselves, as we live with feelings of shame, regret or remorse.

Conversely, when we feel wronged, cheated, violated, or disrespected, it takes great compassion and love to release the all-too-human feelings of anger and hurt, sometimes accompanied by a desire for justification or revenge.

Ultimately, holding onto negative thoughts and energy in either role keeps us locked in the past, making it difficult to move on and express ourselves fully and lovingly to others.

What if we could assume that no one was ever intentionally trying to hurt anyone else?

That's not to say that we should condone harmful behavior, but when we let go of the stories that we tell ourselves about the person or situation, release our judgments and criticisms, and refuse to take on the role of victim, we experience peace and freedom.

Life, whether we define it as good or bad, happens. While we can't undo most circumstances, our quality of life and peace of mind depends on how we perceive a person, situation or event, and how we choose to deal with it. We only have the present moment, and only we get to decide how we are going to experience it. When we can look at ourselves and others with empathy, through a lens of compassion and love, we stand a better chance of creating a kinder, more loving world.

The next story is about a woman who lives each moment with acceptance for what is. For this compassionate woman, forgiveness isn't even a consideration. She lives in the awareness that there's nothing and no one in her life that needs to be forgiven.

Nothing to Forgive

Sophia LaRusso lives her life full-on, with a positive outlook that's as inspiring as it is downright contagious. One would never know that her life has not always been easy.

Oftentimes we don't realize the depth of the human spirit until we hear the story of loss behind it:

"I was the girl from Harlem who married the Italian boy from the Lower East Side. We met while Joseph was a hospital administrator and I was a volunteer," says Sophia. "Our friendship and love story developed into a beautiful marriage of forty-one years."

Everything changed at dusk on the eve of the presidential election in 2008. After waving signs in support of Obama's campaign, Joey (as Sophia lovingly called her husband) was walking across the parkway when he was hit by a car, driven by a young driver who didn't see him.

"Oh, God! This can't be happening!" Sophia cried out as she ran toward her husband, who'd been thrown into the air and landed on his head. As soon as she saw the blood pouring from his eyes and head, she knew he wasn't going to make it. Despite the best efforts of the emergency team, Joey died before reaching the hospital.

Even while experiencing the trauma from the inevitable loss of her husband, Sophia felt compassion for the distraught young driver, who had stayed nearby at the scene of the accident, the entire time. She walked over to him and said, "Your car and you were in the wrong place at the wrong time. It wasn't your fault; it was an accident."

Sophia's faith has kept her strong. "Everyone has a destiny, and we all have a time to die. God gave me this wonderful gift of a loving husband, and it was now time to return that gift. God took my Joey home."

Acknowledging what a treasure he was to their community, three hundred people attended Joseph's "Celebration of Life." Sophia received so many cards each day that she thought the mailman was going to quit his job.

"Joey lived life to the fullest. He was happy, fulfilled, and had no regrets. There was no one for him to forgive, nor was there anyone who needed to forgive him," says Sophia.

Whenever she thinks of the young driver, she doesn't hold him responsible. In fact, months after the accident, she wrote him a letter, saying, "It must be an awful feeling to have a car that has killed someone. Your car was a part of my husband's destiny; you just happened to be behind the wheel. Don't let this fear keep you from driving again. It could have happened to any one of us."

Now, a year later, Sophia says, "Joey's spirit and love surround me every day, and I feel blessed." And she has no fear of death. "No one is going to get out of this life alive! It's what you do when you're breathing, while you're on this side of the grass that matters. What are you leaving? Life is about legacy."

Sophia has impacted many lives through her volunteer work on boards and committees, and for the last three years, Sophia has been mentoring thirteen-year-old Kiana. Their trusting relationship allows them to express their humor freely with each other. On one of their earlier visits, Kiana asked, "Do you know that you're the third mentor I've had because I couldn't relate to any of them?" Sophia quickly responded, "Then we must be the odd couple, because you don't like mentors and I don't like children!" They had a great laugh together. On the night that Sophia lost her husband, Kiana was so concerned that she refused to go to bed until her mom drove her to Sophia's house to make sure that she was alright.

Sophia's philosophy is: "In life, when one door closes, another opens. You can elect to open it, close it, or pretend there's no door. I walk through all doors, and I'm always excited about what's on the other side!"

Thankfully, Sophia believes in opening lots of doors for others to walk through. And she welcomes each person who steps into her life with such love, acceptance, and compassion that there is never any judgment, never anything to forgive.

♡ *Have you ever felt hurt by someone and found it difficult to forgive that person?*

♡ *Were you able to let go of not only the pain, but the anger and resentment toward the other person? How did you do that? How did it make you feel?*

♡ *How do you express your compassion and acceptance of others?*

♡ *Are you able to do that for yourself?*

Seasons of Friendship

Nothing among human things
has such power to keep our gaze
fixed ever more intensely upon God
than friendship.

– Simone Weil

When it comes to friendship, I used to have ideas about what that relationship should look like and how long it should last—usually *forever*—but I've discovered that everyone and everything has its own rhythm. It may match our cadence for a while and then suddenly spin out in a different direction.

When timing and life circumstances bring people together, the connection may feel wonderful until life happens, and people drift apart and move on. It's like the seasons which bring a sense of newness with each transition. I've learned to appreciate and learn from each one.

And then there are those rare friends who never go away. You know they are there even when you can't see them. They love you for who you are, speak their truth while honoring yours, and show up for you as best they can in times of trouble. They are the friends that you can reconnect with after years of not seeing each other and your conversations are as intimate as though you had never spent a moment apart. Or they can be the ones with whom there is an instant connection and comfort level, as though you've been together before, and you know that you will always be a part of each other's lives.

I've come to realize that it's not as important how long you've known each other, nor how you met; what matters is that there is an openness of hearts, a deep level of communication, and a commitment to and an honoring of the friendship. For me, such friendships are a true measure of wealth.

Just as nutritious food is good for the body "nutritious friends" provide nourishment in their relationships. Whether our friendships are short-term or long-lasting, we can ask ourselves: Am I being a "nutritious friend?" Am I fully present and engaged when I am with someone? Do I see and inspire the best in others? When things go awry, as they sometimes will, can I communicate my feelings honestly, with an assumption that no harm was meant by either of us? Am I able to be a loyal friend and be true to myself? How can I comfort my friends when they experience pain and loss? How do I support their dreams and celebrate their successes? Do I express my views and share my world in a positive way? Do my friends feel better after they have spent time with me? Would I want *me* for a friend?

Once in a Lifetime Friend

On a recent three hour flight, I was tempted to keep my nose stuck in a book, but fortunately I chose to engage in conversation with the lovely woman sitting next to me. When I shared the concept of *Love Is the New Currency*, Frankie told me about her friend, Leslie whom she had only known for a short time, but who came to Frankie's aid when she needed it most. This is the story about a "once in a lifetime" friend:

Frankie tried to calm her mind as she sat in the waiting area at the surgery center in Clearwater, Florida, anxious to hear the results of her husband John's surgery. The doctors had told her the procedure was simple, a necessary step prior to the heart-valve-replacement surgery scheduled a couple of weeks later.

Although she had been concerned about John's health for some time, she wasn't prepared for what the doctor told her when he came out of surgery: "Your husband had a massive heart attack. We tried to revive him for 45 minutes … and we weren't successful." In that moment, Frankie's whole world was turned upside down. Now, her best friend and husband of forty-three years was gone.

She had met John when she was only nineteen. He was Canadian and she was from Great Britain; they met while John was attending U.S. Navy Dental Tech School in San Diego. From then on they were a couple. Over the years, they built a successful business and raised a family.

"John was a real romantic and a charmer who had a wonderful spirit of adventure. We did a lot of traveling together," said Frankie. "He liked everyone, and always brought out the best in people. John also brought out the best in me and saw me as a better person than I saw myself. He got me to risk more." She couldn't imagine life without him.

"I was in total shock and just couldn't believe it," says Frankie. "I didn't know who to call, but felt that I couldn't call my kids without planning how I was going to tell them, and making sure that they had someone to support them when they got the news. But I really needed to talk to someone so I just started calling people I knew." After several calls, with no one picking up on the other end, Frankie was grateful to hear Leslie answer the phone.

Leslie and her husband, Edward, lived in Tennessee. John and Edward had been friends for years, but their wives had only recently gotten to know each other. The first time that Leslie and Frankie had met was a year prior, over a half-hour lunch. They didn't see each other again until the two couples had decided to spend six weeks together in a cabin in Tennessee. That vacation was the beginning of a wonderful friendship.

Now Leslie was on the line, and Frankie was finally able to share her loss with someone who cared. Leslie understood Frankie's anguish, having almost lost her own husband a few years earlier. Without hesitation, she told Frankie, "I'll be there by 7:00 tonight. I'm going to call my friend Penny, who lives in Clearwater, and ask her to meet you and to take you home." Frankie was overwhelmed with relief and gratitude.

Within a short time, Penny showed up and made sure that Frankie got home safely. When Frankie thanked her, expecting that she would be leaving to get back to her day, Penny said, "I'm staying with you until Leslie gets here tonight."

When Leslie arrived, Frankie says she couldn't have asked for a better friend to show up for her. "You're not in any shape to be in this house by yourself," Leslie told her, and she arranged to stay with Frankie for two weeks to offer the loving support she clearly needed.

"I was overwhelmed," said Frankie. "It's so hard to lose someone you love who is also your best friend and your life and business partner."

Even now, a year after his death, Frankie finds it hard to believe that her husband is gone. "We used to be able to talk to each other about everything. It's hard not having someone to help me make decisions. I've had to make a lot of adjustments."

Whenever she feels like she's in an "emotional sewer" she's able to pick up the phone and ask for help. Her friend, Dave, who understands the pain of losing a loved one, tells her: "Frankie, it's like waves. They're going to come. All you can do is to get on the raft, hold on tight and ride the waves."

For the most part, Frankie is riding the waves well. "I've gained a lot of confidence in myself and am more outgoing. It has also opened my heart to a whole new world of friendships."

Frankie has found people in whom she can trust and confide in a way that she'd never experienced before. Leslie has proven to be that special kind of friend and their connection only grows stronger. For the last year, Leslie has called Frankie every single day to check on her. She has also flown out on two other important occasions to support Frankie: the memorial service and the acquisition of her U.S. citizenship.

"I've never had such a great friend as Leslie," says Frankie. "It's beyond what I ever understood friendship to be."

♡ *What are the qualities of friendship that you most value?*

♡ *Who are those people in your life whom you consider lifetime friends?*

♡ *How are you a "nutritious friend"?*

♡ *How are you able to show up for a friend in a time of distress?*

Four
Empowerment

And the day came when the risk it took to remain closed in a bud became more painful than the risk it took to bloom.

– Anais Nin

I find that I make my greatest contributions when I'm feeling confident, capable, and valued. Conversely, whenever I'm "living small," plagued with insecurities that limit how I show up in the world, it keeps me from offering my best to others. It doesn't serve anyone well.

There was a time in my life when I didn't value myself or what I had to offer. With little sense of self worth, I allowed someone to verbally push me down until I finally hit bottom. From that vantage point, I had no where to go but up. It became a catalyst for change and the impetus to begin a journey of self-awareness, where I reclaimed all that I had buried—my talents, hopes, and dreams.

I discovered that I was not only resilient, but had an adventurous, open spirit. As a former elementary school teacher, I took a leap of faith to accept a job in wholesale gift sales, having previously only sold Girl Scout cookies.

My job involved driving around in unfamiliar towns and cities and making "cold calls." When I called on clients in resort towns, I was often barely able to afford to pay for the hotel room on my $1200 a month advance (out of which I paid my travel and basic living expenses). But I felt empowered as I developed a new career, and tried things that I had never thought possible … and I thrived.

For four years, I worked hard in a profession that I was passionate about and successful at. I would have continued indefinitely, but things changed abruptly when the company I worked for sold off a "territory"—the one that I had developed. I felt like my foundation was ripped out from underneath me, and I was left with broken dreams and empty pockets. But it gave me the motivation and the freedom to reinvent myself: It was time to start my own company.

Once again, I learned that I could succeed. And not only that, but developing and managing a growing business for the next fifteen years created an opportunity to give others a chance to start a new career and to be empowered by their own success.

Self-Esteem

Be yourself. Everyone else is taken.
– Oscar Wilde

This quote by Oscar Wilde is a great reminder of how special and unique we each are. We offer value to the world when we are fully who we are because no one else can do it better.

But how many of us can stand in front of a mirror and like the person who's looking back? Or is our vision marred by a flurry of "not enoughs"? In a world that is focused on appearances, our tainted filters may show us not pretty enough, thin enough, or tall enough. Or our distorted perceptions can shift to what is invisible to the eye—not good enough, not smart enough.

Why is it that our harshest critic often turns out to be ourselves? Under the guise of helpfulness or humility, we judge what is good, right, or perfect. We're taught in self-help classes and books to build ourselves up by looking in the mirror and saying what it is that we love and appreciate. It reminds me of the popular off-Broadway play, *I Love You, You're Perfect ... Now Change*, only we're saying it to ourselves.

Some people are brought up with a healthy dose of self-esteem, but for others it takes a lot of inner work to acquire that self-assurance. Ultimately, it's up to us to rewrite the script in our heads. We can choose which voices to listen to and what to believe. When we stop comparing ourselves to others, drop the judgments and criticisms, and truly embrace our "shadow side"—all of the things we don't like about ourselves—we often conclude that we aren't so bad after all. We may even like what we see.

The following stories demonstrate ways that people have either successfully transformed their own images or supported others in getting a more kindly view of themselves. They are able to look in the mirror and say, "I love you," and mean it.

"Mirror, Mirror . . ."

When Joe Davinroy was growing up, he wasn't encouraged to see his brilliance. In fact, he was usually put down whenever he had good feelings about himself or when he was proud of an accomplishment, as though self-esteem were a bad thing. He received these messages regularly from his family: "Who do you think you are?" "You shouldn't toot your own horn," and "Boy, are you arrogant!" Although many of his teachers tried to fit him into the "school box image," not seeing or acknowledging his unique talents, there were a few who supported the self-confident, free-spirited and big-hearted boy.

Thirty years and a great deal of inner work later, Joe embraces affirming, positive views of himself and of others. "The biggest thing for me was getting out of victim mode, and realizing that I was responsible for my thoughts and beliefs about myself," Joe says. He remembers a pivotal workshop where he was asked, "Where are you being a victim in your life? How can you be in your power instead?" It launched him into an in-depth search to discover and acknowledge who he is and the special gifts and talents he has to offer.

Joe's generosity is well known in his community. His successful catering business gives him ample opportunities to share what he has learned with the young people who work with him, and to open doors that they never knew existed, just as others had done for him. "If I can do it, anybody can," he says, adding, "Everybody's a teacher, and our experiences, good or bad, are all about learning."

Joe has become a man whom he is pleased to see in the mirror. In fact, a full-length, antique gilded mirror is prominently displayed in his home. Whenever friends are caught up in their insecurities, unable to see their own beauty and light, he lovingly "takes them to the mirror" to have a good look.

Recently, a close friend from out of state was staying with him. "We usually do wall-shaking stuff together, helping each other to look at the negative beliefs we're carrying and then letting them go," Joe says. As his friend was sharing the details of an upcoming audition she was trying out for, she described herself as an old woman trying to tackle something that she hadn't done in twenty years.

"What in the world was I thinking about?" she lamented. "How could I even consider trying out for a part with all of these kids who are so much better than me?"

"Stop," Joe said, as he guided her to the mirror for the "big look" and a chance to see what he saw—her beauty and brilliance. She smiled.

Now there's an ongoing joke between them: Whenever someone is not living up to their potential, the cry is: "Oh, no! NOT the MIRROR!" followed by a good laugh.

♡ *What do you see when you look in your mirror? Do you like what you see?*

♡ *If not, who or what would you like to see reflected in the image?*

♡ *How do your friends give you a different perspective of yourself?*

♡ *What kind of mirror do you hold up to others?*

Getting Her Smile Back

In the search for stories to include in *Love Is the New Currency*, one of the challenges was to convince those who perform acts of kindness, oftentimes anonymously, to share them. For that reason, the participants in this next story have changed their names, wanting only to relate that there are many acts of generosity that take place daily, and that often go unrecognized.

Dr. Ann Tandy, a chiropractor, wanted to support the health of children in her community, and began by offering $10 physicals at a nearby school. At one of these routine screenings, she met a family of four kids who had been referred by a YMCA homeless shelter. Dr. Tandy recommended that they receive free ongoing care at her office. During these treatments, their mom, Debbie, usually stayed in the background, reticent to show her toothless smile.

On one visit, prior to Thanksgiving, Debbie was invited to pick up boxes of food collected by Dr. Tandy and her staff. Bursting into tears over their generosity, she began to feel comfortable enough to share information about herself: "My teeth were knocked out by my ex-husband. I was once a model, but now I don't look attractive. I haven't been able to find employment. I'm lucky when I find jobs driving a cab at night because I have no other way to support my children."

The following week, when Dr. Ken Stewart, a dentist, came into Dr. Tandy's office as a patient, she shared Debbie's story with him, and asked if he knew anyone who could help. Without hesitation, he said, "Send her over."

A team of three doctors and their dental staff worked to give Debbie her smile back. Here is their story, as told by Dr. Stewart's office manager:

When Debbie initially came into our office, she was apprehensive, her face reflecting fear and doubt. She was in so much pain that she couldn't smile.

When Debbie had gone to a dentist a few years earlier, he had refused to treat her because he thought she was a drug addict. She had tried to explain that she had never used drugs, but the dentist still rejected her. Fearful that the same thing would happen again in another dental office, Debbie just gave up on her teeth. She dealt with the pain and learned how to drain the abscesses. When that wasn't successful, she went to the emergency room for treatment.

Debbie was tired of people not taking her seriously, both professionally and personally. She felt helpless to support her four children, and didn't attend functions at her children's school because she was embarrassed about her appearance and was afraid that she would humiliate them. In short, she was at a dead end with no way out.

After Dr. Stewart completed a comprehensive exam, he formulated a treatment plan for her, and sought the help of other dental professionals. An oral surgeon removed all of the hopeless teeth, a total of 14, and then an endodontist did root canal therapy on two more. All of the dentists treated her free of charge.

Once she was pain-free, Debbie was a totally different person. She could smile again; I saw hope in her eyes. And although she has not returned for the final stage of treatment, the doors are open whenever she is ready.

The doctors believe they were given a gift through this experience. "The real reward is not always financial, but it's the joy that one feels in helping someone to turn her life around," says Dr. Stewart. "Gaining self-respect and a new outlook on life sets people free and opens up all types of opportunities both personally and professionally. We are thrilled to be able to give Debbie that chance."

Dr. Tandy, the chiropractor who initiated the process, says, "Not only did Dr. Stewart and two of his colleagues transform the mouth and the life of this woman, what I found amazing was that Dr. Stewart even wrote ME a thank-you note for the referral. I am so honored to know him and his friends, who helped for no glory of their own, but just to be of service."

♡ *Have there been times in your life when you felt as though you were in a rut or at a dead end?*

♡ *What did (or would) change that situation?*

♡ *Have you ever received care for a service you couldn't afford? If so, how did that make you feel?*

♡ *Are there ways that you have empowered others by your care of them?*

Fairy Godmother

Chris Mayer calls herself the Fairy Godmother. She creates real-life Cinderella stories for not just one, but hundreds of girls who may never have gotten to the ball without her help.

It started when Chris, an elementary teacher for thirty-one years, took part in a conversation at a teachers' association meeting. The discussion centered on the depressed economy and the fact that many girls couldn't afford to go to their high school prom due to the expense of buying a dress, shoes, and jewelry. It brought back memories of Chris's own high school proms, when she, too, lacked the money to purchase a gown. Fortunately, her mom was a seamstress, who fashioned creations that made her daughter feel like a real princess.

Chris decided to spearhead an effort to collect prom dresses for girls in the local high schools who couldn't afford to buy one. She anticipated getting 100 or so gowns, most likely older and worn.

What happened when the teachers' union and a community of magnanimous individuals got involved went beyond her wildest dream.

The first person to donate brought in eleven stunning gowns, cleaned and on hangers, many worn only once. Then three boxes arrived full of "drop-dead gorgeous" gowns. As word spread, ten to twenty-five gowns began to arrive daily. Chris received not only gowns, but also "glass slippers"—twenty boxes filled with new designer sandals—as well as jewelry, shawls, purses, makeup, and gift cards for services at hair salons.

What Chris found most heartwarming was the generosity of friends, colleagues, and strangers, people whom these girls would never meet. "Everyone wanted to help to create a magical and memorable experience that the girls would cherish forever. And they did."

An elderly woman, who had saved a beautiful shawl for the daughter she never had, was thrilled to be able to give it to someone who would use it to add the perfect finishing touch for a special occasion.

When Chris discovered that there were not enough gowns of certain sizes, she let it be known that "$15 buys a gown at Goodwill," and received numerous donations totaling $1,200 to purchase the gowns that were still needed.

Chris tutored a teenaged girl, who lived in a country-club neighborhood. The girl's mother was so touched by Chris's vision that she went home and called and e-mailed her friends. An hour later, she came back with twelve exquisite gowns. Through the generosity of her friends, this mother later brought in another seventy-five to one hundred gowns, including some from Scala, Vera Wang, and Versace. Chris said, "They were the most gorgeous gowns that you can imagine, all cleaned and awaiting the princesses who would bring them to life again on the ballroom floor."

When the space in Chris's home overflowed with donations,

friends introduced her to a local dry cleaner, who offered to store and clean the gowns, not realizing that there would be almost 500 of them.

"Cinderella's Closet," as Chris called it, became the center for magical metamorphoses! A day was set aside for the girls to visit, and Chris had a ball (pun intended) as she helped them to select the perfect prom gown and to pin up their hair. No one was turned away. Chris told each girl, "I don't care where you're from. If you need a dress, then take a dress."

Emotions were high as the girls stood in front of the full-length mirror. "Some of them cried as they realized for the first time just how beautiful they were," says Chris. Many girls came with their moms, who were equally touched by the transformation and their daughter's expressions of joy. "We hugged and laughed and cried," Chris says. "And I loved seeing shy, inhibited girls walk in, and confident, beautiful princesses walk out. It was all the thanks I needed." For Chris, this was the "gold."

With a wave of her gilded wand, the Fairy Godmother sent each princess off with a big hug, a boutonniere for their Prince Charming, and a disposable camera to capture her magical fairy tale.

In all, one hundred and forty princesses came to "Cinderella's Closet," and about 250 gowns (size 0 to 26) were given away. Chris says, "Yes, even my size 26 left with a beautiful red chiffon gown, matching shoes, shawl, earrings, and bag. She and her mother looked like they had just hit the lottery! Her principal told this student if she found the dress, he would buy the ticket … and off she went to the ball."

♡ *Have there been times when you looked in the mirror and felt unattractive? What helped to change that perception?*

♡ *How are you able to support another in seeing their beauty or worth?*

♡ *What was your experience in going to a prom or a ball? Did you feel transformed?*

♡ *Are there ways that you could share the things that make you feel special with others?*

Jump Start

> *Why wait? Life is not a dress rehearsal.*
> *Quit practicing what you are going to do, and just do it.*
> *In one bold stroke you can transform today!*
>
> — Phillip Markens

A little over a year ago, I was surprised to learn that my godfather, Uncle Fred, had another godchild, Trudy Paine, who owned a vintage clothing store in a college town in Massachusetts. I discovered that connection after Trudy had mentioned to my mom that she was in the market for vintage dresses. Wanting to clear her attic of the sentimental things stored by her three long-grown children, my mom called to ask me, "Would you be interested in selling your prom dress?"

I was disconcerted. "Seriously? My sexy prom dress, slit up the sides, with hot pants, is now considered VINTAGE?" Apparently so.

A few months later, I got to meet Trudy, the woman who eventually sold this irreplaceable vestige of my fashionable past, at the funeral service of our godfather. It was a wonderful meeting, despite the sad circumstances, and I sent out a thought of gratitude to Uncle Fred for this new connection in my life. In fact, Trudy and I now refer to each other as "godsisters."

When I mentioned that I was writing a book about people

who were touching the lives of others, Trudy said, "I have a great story for you!" Told in her own words, here is what took place one afternoon at Uncle Margaret's Vintage Clothing Store:

Wonder how much money I'll make today? I thought, grappling with a crossword puzzle while I awaited customers. It was a very slow day at my store, and the entire street seemed eerily quiet— even the birds weren't making a sound.

I heard a shuffle outside, and looking out the store window, I saw a lanky young man with long, spaghetti-like legs slowly walking toward the front door. His shoulders were stooped, his head was hanging, and he seemed to be staring more at the ground than at his destination.

Hmmmm. This will be interesting.

The young man entered the store and stood in front of the counter. He didn't make eye contact. "Hi. I've been looking for work, and wonder if you're hiring, but I suppose you're not, so I guess I'll leave."

He looked so defeated standing there in his worn-out clothes and downcast demeanor.

Impulsively, I pointed to the men's dressing room and said, "Wait a minute. Go into that room." Then I grabbed a pair of black pants, a 1950s blue suit jacket, and a shirt that all looked like they would fit, and handed them to him. "Try these on just for fun."

"Okay," he said, looking puzzled, but passively responding to my directive. As he shuffled to the room, I heard him mumble, "Sure, why not. I haven't got anything better to do."

A few minutes later, he emerged from the dressing room. I couldn't believe the metamorphosis. "Go look at yourself in the mirror," I ordered.

When he did, it was like watching a dry, droopy flower get some raindrops. He straightened his posture, his eyes brightened, and his mouth fell open. "Wow! Everything fits perfectly," he said, looking pleased with what he saw.

As I approached him to straighten his shirt collar, he appeared a bit perplexed. I looked into his eyes and said, "Now, go look for work!"

"But I can't afford these clothes," he said.

"Yes, you can. Once when I was younger, I got help from a truck driver who told me to pass it on, and so I am. You do the same thing."

Then I put his other clothes in a bag, handed it to him, and pointed to the door. "Go on. Git." After saying thank you a dozen times, he walked confidently out of the store.

I looked out the window and watched as he started walking faster. Then something magical happened. He jumped up, clapped his heels together, threw his arms in the air, and snapped his fingers. Through teary eyes, I laughed, seeing his spontaneous joy.

About two-and-a-half hours later, he came running into the store. Panting and out of breath, he said, with a wide grin, "I had to come to tell you: I got a job! A REAL job!"

"Good for you," I said, giving him a high five.

After he left, I realized that what he'd given me that day was worth far more than making a sale. He accepted my gesture of giving, he shared his young adult world with me, and unbeknownst to him, he reminded me that connecting to another human being with kindness makes everyone involved feel good.

He also left me with a beautiful memory that I pull out whenever I need a lift, and it immediately makes me smile.

♡ *Are there times when you are "living small," not living up to the potential of who you are meant to be?*

♡ *Have you ever shifted your perspective of yourself because of the way that someone else saw you?*

♡ *What are the day to day things that you can do to help others to see their potential and their gifts?*

Laying a Foundation

*"The life I touch for good or ill will touch another life,
and that in turn another, until who knows where the trembling
stops or in what far place my touch will be felt."*

– Frederick Buechner

Jan, a successful and self-assured client, once shared with me that she had no real family until a kind and generous man took on the responsibility of raising her and several orphans. He provided for their education, took them on trips throughout the world, and offered them an expansive vision of what was possible in their lives. Most importantly, he created a family and gave them a place to call home.

"It was like having a maypole, this solid center from which I could venture out, try new things, and yet always feel that I had a connection to something and someone besides myself," said Jan.

I've often thought of this image and how it translated in my own life. I was blessed with a loving family, who gave me a strong foundation, my maypole. Although my parents had not graduated from high school, they encouraged and helped me to go to college, the first in my family to do so. They had never traveled and had always lived in the same town, yet they supported my vision of living in new places to expand my world.

In my late twenties, after separating from my husband, I moved back with my parents for a few months. During this time and despite the fact that I had never lived alone before, I made a decision to move to a state that I had never been to, about 1900 miles away from my hometown, with no job and no place to live. After saying a tearful goodbye to my parents, I drove with a friend to Colorado in a Ford Pinto. (You may remember it—the one with the exploding gas tank!) With me, I had only my bicycle, clothes, a two-person tent that I had learned to put up the night before, and a little cash.

Shortly after my arrival in Colorado, I wrote a letter to my parents to thank them for believing in me, for not talking me out of something that may have seemed risky or foolish, but that I felt compelled to try, and for having the faith that I would do well. (Of course, my dad, who likes to joke, threatened to sell their home, move, and forget to send me their new address!) I'm grateful for their faith in me when even I wasn't sure where this act of pure intuition would lead me.

The next two stories are about individuals who chose to guide and support the children who were brought into their lives. These mentors created a maypole for each child, holding a vision of what was possible until, one by one, the children could find their wings and fly.

An Adoring Fan

There's a glow that emanates from some people, a peaceful presence that you want to bask in. Kate has that radiance. "I love my life," she says. "Things are never bad. Even in the midst of chaos, I believe that there's some kind of order to it all. I find what helps is being and doing my best to benefit other people and myself."

A single mom with modest means, Kate has never felt a sense of lack. "I don't need that much. I keep giving money, time, and resources away and it keeps coming back tenfold. I can live on relatively little and enjoy it."

When I invited Kate to share her mentoring experiences in *Love Is the New Currency*, she was reticent, saying, "I don't have anything unique to contribute." In her varied roles as school counselor, Big Sister, and social worker, Kate has found what she considers "the most uplifting work." She adds, "It's so great when you find what you are meant to do in your life, and mine is human service, serving others."

How do you measure the impact on even one child who will live a more balanced and expansive life because of their interactions with you? Kate has helped many students over the years, but her relationship with one little girl stands out:

Ten years ago, Kate was working as a school counselor when she met a third-grader named Jen, who was learning-disabled and emotionally handicapped. Jen knew a lifesaver when she met one; she latched onto Kate and never let go.

The other children would often avoid Jen with her matted hair and mildewed smell. Once, when she was not allowed back in school because of a lice infestation, Kate was able to get permission from her normally absent mother to get Jen's hair cut. She even used her own money to buy medicine to treat her.

Jen loved Kate and treasured whatever time they could spend together, which became regular once Kate decided to take her on as a Little Sister through the Big Brothers Big Sisters program. "Jen is a remarkable girl with such resiliency," Kate says. "She's a survivor and has high self-esteem, despite the fact that she lives in a trailer with most of the floorboards missing and has nothing to call her own, except the responsibility for her younger siblings."

Although Kate was always willing to help, she was amazed that Jen never asked for anything. On one shopping trip, Kate offered to buy whatever she needed, and Jen chose an inexpensive mascara and a pair of flip-flops. One cold winter day, Kate gave her a cozy blue blanket to keep warm. Ten years later, Jen still talks about that gift.

Kate believes that every child needs an adoring fan, someone to express wild enthusiasm for her accomplishments. With this kind of support, Jen went from getting D's and F's in school to finishing some years later with A's, B's, and C's.

Jen and her siblings were eventually taken away from their mother, who was addicted to crack, and were placed in the custody of their father. A few years later, when Jen's dad lost his job, he decided to move his family several states away. Kate managed to gather money to buy gift cards for gas and food to help with their travel expenses.

Once Kate happened to run into Jen's mom as she was about to board a bus. Kate went up to her and said, "I just want you to know that even though you can't see your kids, they still love you." The only mother-daughter photo Jen's mom has is the one Kate had taken of the two of them.

Jen recently turned eighteen. She told Kate she is hopeful about her life, especially when she can leave home and be on her own. Jen has no money of her own, but Kate has been putting aside the money that would have been spent during their get-togethers and holidays, over the year they had been apart, and had saved $400 to help Jen start a new life. Jen's first purchase will be a cell phone so that she and Kate can communicate more often.

Jen's goal is to continue with her schooling and become a teacher. Although they live about a thousand miles apart, Kate says, "I plan to go to her graduation, and to help her as best as I can to manifest a dream of getting a degree in education. I'm so proud of Jen and all that she's become."

♡ *Is there a way that you could be an adoring fan of a child that would give her/him a feeling of being loved and valued?*

♡ *Would you be willing to give an hour of your time monthly to support the well-being of a child in your neighborhood, family, or church group?*

♡ *What unique gift or message would you want to share with that child?*

Footprints

As a young African-American girl growing up in a low-income housing project, Alice didn't know about dreams and goals. No one was around when she got home from school to ask how her day was or to care whether she did her homework. It was all that her single mom could do to put food on the table and a roof over the heads of her three growing children.

If anyone had asked Alice what she wanted to be when she grew up, she would have responded, "I want to be a maid, just like my mom." She remembers the first time she went with her mom to clean the big, beautiful homes in a neighboring area; she thought she'd "died and gone to heaven." She hadn't known that such a way of life existed. Alice watched as her mother cleaned these mansions barefoot, so she wouldn't leave any shoe prints on the carpet. "She was very proud of her work," says Alice. I had thought, *It's what I'm supposed to do.*

Although her father was rarely present, he was the love of Alice's life. "My papa was a rolling stone. Wherever he put his head down was where he called home." At the age of nine, she witnessed her father being shot by one of his many girlfriends. He survived, but was paralyzed and wheelchair-bound. Even then he was rarely around, yet Alice still cherished every moment that she had with him.

Alice got pregnant at twenty and became a mom at twenty-one. "I followed in my mother's footsteps; all I knew was how to work and make ends meet," she says. "There was little or no time to be involved in my son's life."

It wasn't until she got laid off from a job she loved that Alice asked herself what she wanted to do with her life. Not knowing the answer, she decided to enroll in a community college with the help of financial aid. "I felt proud to be able to say I was going to college, and was frequently commended for my good work."

A flexible schedule and free time gave Alice an opportunity

to be the kind of parent that she had always wanted to be. She says, "The most gratifying moment of my life was when I became a mother to my son, just as he was getting ready to go to middle school. I finally was able to open my son's backpack and know what I needed to know to help him. It was the first time that we sat at the kitchen table together to do his homework. And I got to see the excitement in his eyes and hear, 'Mom, look what I got!' as he showed me a good grade."

Alice began volunteering at her son's school, and realized that many parents were unable to be there for their children. She asked her son how many of his friends needed help with their homework. She started assisting six youngsters, driving them to the library to study after school. Later, she was offered an empty computer room in the community center and she opened it to ten kids who came to study every day. "I wanted to do my best, not only for my son, but for all of them. It gave me hope. I believed that I could make a difference, and they believed in me."

In 2005, Alice started a nonprofit organization, *Brothers and Sisters Doing the Right Thing.* In addition to after-school and Saturday tutoring, it provides summer recreational and educational programs for teens to encourage service and leadership skills.

Alice shares how easy it is now for her to ask and involve others in her goal of giving "her kids" new life experiences. She smiles as she relates how she just stopped in one day at an exclusive tennis resort—in the very neighborhood where her mom had cleaned houses—to share her vision of creating a Fantasy Island Adventure for these teens. The management loved the idea.

Two rooms were set aside for the boys and girls to use as changing rooms. "You should have seen the look on each one's face as an individual key to a hotel room was put into their hands," says Alice. The kids had a blast as they lived out their fantasy adventure: enjoying a specially prepared lunch, swimming in a luxurious pool, participating in a tennis clinic, and even touring the kitchen, furthering the dream of two young boys who wanted to become chefs. Alice says, "It was heartwarming to see these kids enjoy what, for many of them, was the best day of their lives."

It's not just about fun. Recently, the owner of a successful real estate firm created a week-long entrepreneurship program for the teens. Business professionals came to share their experiences and to answer questions. The young people learned rules of etiquette and were taken to a restaurant to dine.

"Most of these kids had never explored life beyond the ten square blocks of their neighborhood. Oftentimes their only way out was through football scholarships, if they were good enough," says Alice. "Now, they are being supported to go inside and find out what it is they really want. Unless they can feel, touch and taste it … it's just a dream."

Once, when funding was short, a little girl said to Alice: "Don't be like everyone else. Don't start something and quit." Quitting is the furthest thing from Alice's mind. In fact, she is launching a new program called *Let Our Voices Be Heard*, introducing the students to politics and the power of the written word.

Recently, Alice learned something of her own history that deeply resonated with her. Her great-grandmother, Elizabeth Black Owens, was so determined that her own children and others from her neighborhood would have an education that she loaded them into her station wagon and drove them to the "school for children of color." She later went on to become a minister and pastor of a church. Mrs. Owens was honored in the Visionary Women of 2001 Exhibit as part of the Venice Foundation and the Venice Archives and Area Historical Collection.

Without realizing it, Alice was following in the footsteps of her own lineage of powerful women. She has come a long way from the young girl who was taught to erase her footprints in the carpet. Alice empowers others by supporting their visions and encouraging them to leave their own unique footprints in the world.

♡ *Have you ever followed in the footsteps of a family member or someone you admired?*

♡ *How have you made your own mark in the world?*

♡ *Are there ways in which you can make meaning of your own journey by creating a path for others to follow?*

Unshakable Belief

Sometimes our light goes out but is blown into flame
by another human being.
We owe deepest thanks to those who have rekindled this light.
— Albert Schweitzer

Have you ever had someone in your life who held an unshakable belief in you? That person didn't lose faith no matter how often you failed or how many times you stopped trying. It may have been a parent, relative, teacher or friend who recognized your potential, saw the best in you, and upheld that vision until you could own it.

It's never too late to be transformed by someone's belief in us—no matter how old we are or how ingrained our negative image. And once we reach our goals and fulfill our dreams, we can turn around and hold that belief for someone else.

David Rubin has an exquisitely kind and generous way of seeing the best in others, while inspiring them to reach beyond their perceived limitations. He believes "Everyone has a unique gift and a contribution to make. The key is to discover what it is."

When asked about his upbringing and what it is that motivates him to hold a positive view of others, David said, "My parents always believed in my brother and me. Over the years, we tried lots of businesses that failed, but our parents never gave up. They continued to support us financially, believing that we would one day 'get it,' and they never lost patience. Although we were considered smart guys, we were late bloomers—it wasn't until we were well into our forties that we found our niche and created what has become a successful business."

Whenever David meets people who are struggling, he wonders if they have had a family who believed in them or a good support system. "I had help, which made a huge difference. I can't repay the debt to my parents, I can only pay it forward."

David and his wife Adie are generous, not only in what they give, but in how they show up for others. Their *currency of love* is appreciation, acknowledgement, and respect for each person they meet. You know that you are seen and heard when you are with them.

The following story, told in David's own words, is a beautiful example of how individuals are able to see the wondrousness in others, and to hold on to that belief until they can see if for themselves—no matter what.

Transforming a Life

Give a man a fish and you feed him for a day.
Teach a man to fish and you feed him for a lifetime.

— Chinese Proverb

The first time I met James, he was working at an off-price clothing chain. My wife, Adie, and I were in the men's department, and James was moving clothes from one rack to another. There was something so ill-at-ease, so uncomfortable about him. He was painfully intense, as though he was one moment away from breaking. Adie and I looked at each other and, feeling the awkwardness, decided to leave the store and move on to our other chores.

When we got outside, we shared a "Wow, that was intense" moment. Then Adie said, "I'll be right back." I was sure she was going to complain to the manager about the young man. After waiting impatiently outside the store for ten minutes, I went in after her. She wasn't with the manager after all. Adie was standing three feet from the young man, looking into his eyes, talking to him. I watched from the store entrance, so proud of Adie for her compassion.

As practicing Buddhists, we are taught to honor and respect each human life, and to make it our highest calling to help even one person to break through their suffering and live a life of joy and hope. Adie was giving me a lesson in how to do that.

And thus began our relationship with James. We shared our Buddhist practice with him, and he took to it instantly. He soon began making great strides in his daily life—earning his driver's license, putting a down payment on a car, getting his GED. But inwardly, James was still suffering. Worst of all, he sought relief in alcohol. We would get calls from him every few days, his voice cracking and his language slurred. He would do everything he could to undermine his forward progress—drink himself into a stupor, miss classes, and miss work.

At these times, we would head over to his house, help clean him up, get some coffee into him, and head home. It was a ritual that we would repeat many times. James soon moved to Vermont to live closer to his brother, but my relationship with him continued. He was in and out of jobs and seemed unable to stick with any path. He was constantly plagued by feelings of being disrespected by everyone around him, and he became increasingly more isolated from others. He was virtually unemployable.

I have been fortunate in my life to have people who believed in me before I believed in myself. Now, whenever I meet someone who doesn't have that someone to believe in them, a bell goes off in my head. Or, perhaps I should say, it goes off in my heart. What greater gift can there be than to have the opportunity to repay my debts of gratitude to those who helped me along the way?

I was determined to help James to win in his life, and so I took an unusual step: I decided to cover his expenses for one year. I wanted to give him time to take a deep breath, collect himself, get some counseling, and rejoin the working world. I simply would not give up on him. Just as the year came to an end, James took a position as an apprentice to a well-known dog trainer. It was hard work and a lot was expected of him. The stress of the job and the no-nonsense approach of his boss proved to be too much for him. He began to drink and was soon fired.

But, almost magically, a seed had been planted: James had discovered that he loved working with dogs. It was as though a light turned on inside of him. He was homeless, cold, and unemployed, but for the first time in his life, he had a mission: to work with dogs. Dogs give unconditional love. Dogs don't talk down to you. Dogs don't judge you. It was a match made in heaven.

We connected James with a counselor friend of ours who lived near him and, for the first time, James found himself in an environment in which he could begin the slow process of re-entering the world. He entered a therapeutic program and started attending all of his required sessions. He connected with a local Buddhist group. He started to encourage others who had lost their way. He stopped drinking. But most importantly, James found a calling.

James is now successfully growing a dog-care business in Vermont, where he offers a wide range of services to dog owners, including walking, sitting, transportation, and training. After years of being foiled by simple administrative tasks, he now glides through new computer programs, bookkeeping applications, website building— everything he needs to build his new business. The accolades are pouring in from his growing clientele.

My philosophy of giving is to "teach someone how to fish." To me, helping someone to become self-reliant is the best gift I can give. It doesn't mean that they don't still need people. We all do. It means that they have the basic means to pay for their place on the planet ... it's a symbol to them that they belong here.

Today James is proud, responsible, and happy. And he has been sober for sixteen months. On more than one occasion, James has written to us to say how profoundly grateful he is. As he put it: "If I live for a thousand years, I could never repay my debt of gratitude to you and Adie for coming back into the store to talk to me. You saved my life."

♡ *Have you ever encountered someone who was so negative that you just wanted to get away? How did you respond?*

♡ *How could you support someone to change an unkindly view they hold of themselves?*

♡ *Have there been times when you were acting in a way that pushed others away?*

♡ *How did you want them to respond to you?*

Quitting Is Not an Option

The only child of a successful football coach in New England, Joan Bellisimo learned at an early age that in order to get somewhere, you need to work hard. Her dad was a great role model not only for his daughter, but for the many kids he coached. He never let anybody quit if he had anything to do with it. If ever Joan wanted to stop doing a project because she was tired of it, she knew what her dad would say: "We don't quit. When you sign on to do something, you need to persevere until it's done. Do the best you can, just because you can." These messages served her well throughout her life, and especially, when, as an adult, she went through a personal tragedy and wanted to give up.

In 2004, Joan moved to Florida and became a tennis pro at a small tennis club, where she met two sisters, Kellee and Kim, as well as two of their friends, who had been playing tennis together for almost fifteen years. She volunteered to take over the weekly nighttime classes and quickly grew to love this close-knit group.

Nine months later, Joan's partner of eight years died suddenly. Joan was devastated. "I was robotic, going through the motions, filled with an emotional emptiness that I couldn't fill," she said. "In those darkest moments, these women whom I'd just met came to my rescue. Kellee and Kim threw me a lifeline and kept me participating and present in everyday life." Holidays and weekends were especially tough, but they always made sure Joan had somewhere to go. She believes that if it weren't for this network of friends she might not be here. And she's never forgotten their compassion, which became the impetus for change in all of their lives.

As the months passed, Joan is the first to admit that she has become a different person. "When I was growing up, I was a spoiled brat," she says. "When I gave or did something for someone, it was whatever was easy for me to do. Now, I can't do or give enough to others, and I'm honored to do it."

When the popular weight-loss TV show *The Biggest Loser* hit the screen, Joan and Kellee would dissect each show, season after season. Joan says, "I loved Jillian's (one of the hosts) training style. She was outspoken, ruled with an iron fist, and would not take any excuses for not following the regimen. At that time, Kellee, who weighed 326 pounds, promised me that if she won the lottery, I could be her 'Jillian' forever."

One day, Kellee announced that she was going to have lap band surgery, which would reduce the capacity of her stomach to take in food. Although Joan was scared for her, Kellee was so committed that Joan jumped on board asking, "When do we start?"

With hesitation, Kellee responded, "What do you mean?"

"When do I get to be your 'Jillian'? Joan asked.

Again there was a hesitation, so Joan said, "Let's just put this right on the table. There will never be any talk of money. I am your trainer." Joan had found a way to give back.

And so, eight weeks after surgery, Joan and Kellee started training. They began at 5:45 a.m., three days a week, with a routine that consisted of running (actually shuffling) for ten seconds and walking for twenty. Days later, at the completion of their first half mile, both women cried tears of joy.

Kellee Bauser shares what the experience of working with her "Jillian" was like:

"If you're lucky enough to have someone in your life to help you shoot for the moon, then there is no way you can fail. I happen to have just such a person in mine. Joan is my friend, mentor, life coach, tennis instructor, and personal fitness trainer, who truly believes in me. She saw something in me early on and was 'all in'. We began with baby steps, literally running from one mailbox to the next in my neighborhood. I had this amazing person who was giving me the gift of her time. No way was I letting her or myself down. Selflessness is truly motivational. Exactly seven months after my surgery, I ran a community four-mile run—36,000 seconds in a row, no walking! I wasn't fast and it wasn't pretty, yet there was Joan, running the entire race backward to keep me centered and focused."

Joan couldn't be prouder of Kellee. "When I think of Kellee today, my heart is full of love and total admiration for all she has done to change her life. There are athletes, gifted athletes, and then there are Olympic athletes. Kellee is an Olympian in her spirit, determination, and effort. I tell her, 'Kellee Bauser, you're my hero.'"

Kellee started to look so good that her sister, Kim, Kim's daughter, and her other friends committed to working with Joan too. A Wednesday night, drop-in boot camp was added to the weekly routine. "Our equipment is limited and our space is small, but their spirit is larger than life," says Joan. "Kellee inspires them all and lets them know that they can do anything they want to if they're willing to work at it. She never complains about being pushed by her 'Jillian.' Her trust in me, and in herself, is boundless."

Kellee has lost 145 pounds in a year and a half and is not stopping there. "There's no exercise too hard, no run too long, no obstacle that I can't overcome to achieve what I want out of life," Kellee says. "There's nothing I can't do or at least try."

Joan beams, just as her dad might have done, upon hearing the words that mean *quitting is not an option.*

♡ *Do you have someone in your life who holds an unshakable belief in you? How does that make you feel?*

♡ *Is there someone you know who could benefit from your positive belief in them?*

♡ *How could you empower that person to be more of who they want to be?*

♡ *How can you acknowledge and celebrate the unique gifts and qualities of others, as well as your own?*

Five
Body, Mind, and Spirit: A Human Experience

We are spiritual beings having a human experience.
— Pierre Teilhard de Chardin

Life can be difficult, and it's not always fair, but overall, I consider it a privilege to be having this human experience.

Even though at one time or another, we will all face health challenges, the painful loss of loved ones, and eventually the demise of our own body, it's awe-inspiring to love and be loved, to have the ability to touch, hear, smell, taste, see and experience the richness of life: the wonder and beauty of nature, the closeness of a lover, good food, music, conversation, and connections.

One of the greatest gifts of being human is the ability to receive and to express love. Our heart expands when we witness the birth of a new life, the tenderness of a couple who have been together for decades, or people's everyday expressions of love and kindness. And if you've ever felt chills, goose bumps, (or *god bumps*, as some people call them) you know that you have heard, seen or experienced something profound, a deep truth that resonates within your very being. Whenever that happens to me, I stop to take it in, grateful to be alive and able to be so deeply moved.

I haven't always appreciated being in this body. There was a time in my life when I wanted to run away from myself, but realized I would have to *take me with me*. After a period of time, following numerous inner and outer conversations, reading, meditating, reflecting and being in touch with my core essence, I came across the title of a book, *Wherever You Go, There You Are* (by Jon Kabat-Zinn), and I let out a peaceful sigh. The title resonated with me; I knew that I was not only at home in this body, but I would be able to lovingly show up for myself.

Perhaps one way to measure our worth is how we show up for ourselves and for others. Despite all of our frailties, insecurities, and faults, when we choose to open to love and to our *oneness* and say "yes" to what opens the door to others, it empowers us and gives significance to our existence.

This chapter is a celebration of the human body, mind and spirit—our common humanity. It offers examples of how people are learning to take care of themselves and each other in challenging life circumstances, while finding acceptance and meaning in the experience.

Self-Care

I say yes when I mean no
and the wrinkle grows.
– Naomi Shihab Nye

Self-care is an act of kindness. How can we take care of anyone else if we don't care for ourselves first? The airlines understand this and tell passengers, "In case of an emergency, if the oxygen masks drop, put your own mask on first before assisting children or others."

If we're healthy, balanced, and feel good about ourselves, we not only have more to give to others, but we have a better chance at connecting on a deeper level. Self-care implies loving and accepting ourselves without criticism and judgment. It can also mean that sometimes we have to say no to others in order to be true to ourselves. When we do things out of love and joy, rather than obligation, we are much happier. And we can then support others to take care of themselves and be happier, too.

When we take the time to do what nourishes us, when we plan our day to include time for ourselves and the things that we love, we feel better and are less stressed. But we need to make it a priority or it doesn't happen. For instance, when was the last time that you made a date with yourself … and kept it?

Loving ourselves, living consciously, and listening to our body's messages before illness or injury forces us to pay attention are important aspects of self-care.

Like many of us, perhaps you may have been conditioned to believe that you should always come last, that your needs aren't as important as those of everyone else, or that it's selfish to think of yourself.

That was true of Linda Maree, the oldest of six children, who grew up believing that she had to take care of others before considering her own needs, if at all. As an adult, she supported her bosses by working long hours, drinking a pot of coffee daily just to keep going. It wasn't until she had a life threatening illness, that she made a decision to take care of herself. "The first time I was hospitalized I realized I had to make some changes in my lifestyle, and I did. But it wasn't enough. The second time I was hospitalized for the same condition, my doctors told me that major surgery was my only option. It was then I made the decision to put my health first, before anything else."

These days, Linda is her own boss and more diligent about balancing work and rest. And she has let go of the message that she received as a child, "Don't be so picky," whenever she was hesitant about eating certain foods. She has avoided surgery and carefully selects everything she puts into her body. Coffee is only an occasional treat and her diet is loaded with organic vegetables and other healthy foods. While Linda used to be concerned about the cost of buying organic, today she considers it a priority to make purchases that support her well-being. "I finally decided I was worth it," she says. "And I have more to give others when I am also giving to myself."

I've also had one of those dramatic wake-up calls, although mine was more of a smack to the head (an effective way to get the attention of an Aries), which caused me to shift my thinking and priorities. During the height of my workaholic years (prior to the peaceful time that I mentioned earlier), I was consistently working 60 to 80 hours a week. At one point, I was preparing for my company's 10-year anniversary celebration, as well as a major gift show, and had just hired a new sales manager. Two days before the show started, I decided to gift myself with an hour massage. After it was finished, in a rush to get back to work, I jumped off of the massage table and ran smack into the sharp corner of a wall, giving myself a mild concussion. The massage therapist invited me to rest there while she went to lunch. When she returned, I sat up and just cried and cried. It was the wake-up call that I needed to realize how poorly I was taking care of myself.

I was reminded of what I once told a friend: "I think of my body like a car. It gets me where I need to go. I feed it, water it, fix it when it doesn't work well, but I don't relate to it on a personal level."

Later, as I reflected on that statement, I asked myself, *If I were a car, what kind of a car would I be?* I felt like the stable car that I was driving: a Volvo, "but I'm evolving to a red Jaguar convertible," I'd say. It made for great dinner and party conversation. A friend even gave me a toy version of the red convertible for my birthday.

Although I never made the leap to a Jaguar, I did make the choice to be kind to myself—to pay attention, to appreciate, and to care for my body, mind, and spirit, keeping myself healthy as best as I can for as long as I'm able.

♡ *Are you loving or critical when you talk to yourself?*

♡ *In taking care of others, do you include your own needs?*

♡ *How do you appreciate, acknowledge or comfort yourself?*

♡ *Do you keep the promises that you make to yourself?*

Transforming Illness

Tell me what it is you plan to do with your one
wild and precious life.

— Mary Oliver

While most of us find it difficult to keep our spirits up when we're sick or injured, fortunately, it's oftentimes a temporary situation resolved by naturopathic or allopathic remedies, along with a lot of sleep, fluids, and loving care.

I remember feeling fragile and vulnerable after fracturing my shoulder. There were many things that I couldn't do, yet it was difficult to be dependent on others for basic needs. I was forced to let go of the incessant *doingness*, extremely difficult for a Type A personality. But thankfully, the injury was short-term, and during the months of healing, I learned a more balanced and peaceful way of living life that has served me well.

But how do any of us deal with an illness that has become a permanent part of our life and is causing us to redefine who we are? Whether it comes as a surprise or as a slow evolvement, when we can no longer deny that our body is not the same as it once was, nor will it ever be, we face a challenge in accepting a card that we didn't want or expect to be dealt. It can be challenging to maintain a positive outlook.

For example, how do we deal with a diagnosis of a serious illness without feeling that our body has betrayed us? How do we relate to the world when we feel less than whole and have to pretend that everything is okay? It's difficult to interact with others who may not want to see us as vulnerable or less than perfect when we can hardly handle that thought ourselves.

How do we see the blessings rather than blame God, others, or ourselves for a life situation that will never end as long as we are attached to our body? How do we experience ourselves as loveable when we feel like a shadow of our former selves, or when we fear being a burden to others?

The following story is about a woman who bravely faced her illness and addressed such questions and fears. She has redefined who she is as a loving, functioning human being, choosing to live her life fully, while helping others to do the same. Dora Briegleb and others like her are life's quiet, everyday heroes.

Playing Her Cards Well

Born in Greece to an aristrocratic mother and a peasant father, Dora found it natural to be open-minded toward a variety of people and life experiences. She was loved unconditionally and allowed to follow her heart with total freedom. At seventeen, her adventuresome spirit took her to the United States to attend college. The following year, she did what she considered "the wildest thing she had ever done"—she married her American sweetheart, Bruce. It worked out beautifully. The couple raised two daughters and their marriage is still going strong after thirty-six years.

Dora developed a personal relationship with God while she was in her twenties. That faith has been her guiding light, and has helped her endure her greatest personal challenge—an encounter with cancer.

"Cancer is the best and the worst thing that's ever happened to me," says Dora. "When I was first diagnosed, I felt like my body had betrayed me. I looked at it with suspicion, as though it were the enemy. I was scared. It triggered fears about my own mortality." Throughout her journey of a double mastectomy, six months of chemo, and eight years of hormonal therapy, she researched and learned a great deal. She discovered that there's no cure for breast cancer and it could reappear at any time. She says, "It's made every day precious. My experience was positive, despite it being a life-threatening disease."

The help and prayers that Dora has received from people, including strangers, has made her want to give back by helping others to get through their healing process with more ease.

Dora had learned that making lifestyle changes, particularly increasing her physical activity and being in a support group, could greatly increase her chances for survival. "I didn't want that information to be wasted," she says, so for the last twelve years, Dora has been the volunteer program coordinator of "TeamSurvivor" in Boulder, Colorado. There, she leads groups of cancer survivors through weekly activities such as walking, dancing, lifting weights, yoga, and, depending on the weather, hiking, snowshoeing, rock climbing, and swimming. They even go on fun trips.

"While joining is not for everyone," Dora says, "those who participate find that they are part of a community, that they are not alone, that people come to cheer them on, and that there are others who have walked in their shoes and who understand how they feel. When you see someone else do well, you think, *I can do it too!*"

In her search to reclaim and maintain her health, Dora spent years in education and fitness training, and developed core exercise programs to assist others. She's quick to spot and to help someone in need. In one fitness class that Dora attended, she noticed a woman in her mid-forties who was bald. She went up to her and said, "I used to be bald," and invited her to join their group of survivors. Three years later, this woman thanked Dora: "You saved my life."

"The essence of Dora is happiness and helpfulness," says her friend Peg. "She reaches out to everyone who has the "C" word. She connects people beautifully."

Through the last twelve years, Dora has had to lose her old self in order to create a *new normal.* She says, "I give myself permission to let some things go in my life that don't really matter and devote myself to those things that really do matter. I don't go back to living my life flippantly. I only have today, and I'm thankful for every minute. Sometimes life deals you cards you don't want, but what you can do is play them well."

And Dora plays hers beautifully—with gumption, gratitude, and grace.

♡ *Have you ever had an accident or an illness that left you feeling vulnerable?*

♡ *How were you able to maintain a sense of yourself, while allowing others to help you?*

♡ *Were you able to find a place of gratitude during such a challenging life situation?*

♡ *How can you share your experience to help others with an illness to find peace with their "new normal"?*

Peaceful Passing

In the end, everyone is aware of this:
Nobody keeps any of what he has,
and life is only a borrowing of bones.

– Pablo Neruda

For most people death is one of their greatest fears. Few of us want to think about what will happen when our body stops functioning and the person that we have thought ourselves to be is no longer walking on this Earth. Our fears may be even more poignant when a loved one is dying.

An antidote to the fear of death, subscribed to by many people, is a strong faith in a power greater than ourselves and a belief that our souls continue.

Regardless of one's religious or spiritual beliefs, a prescription for tranquility is to live fully in the moment, loving and appreciating whom we are with and what we are engaged in.

I remember reading the following brief but memorable encounter. It's become a way for me to check in to the present moment and ask whether I am happy and content with what I am doing.

> One day, as St. Anthony was hoeing in his garden, someone came up to him and asked: "What would you do if you were told that you would die tomorrow?" Without hesitation, he replied: "I would continue hoeing in my garden."

Ah, to have such peace. What would it be like to have nothing on our "to-do" list except to simply be, calmly accepting that all that we are and all that we have could be gone in a moment? This awareness provides a good formula for living.

A dear friend, Bob Keck, was serene throughout his dying process, which lasted a few months. Although he was concerned about and sad to leave his wife Diana, "the love of my life," and his family and friends, he was able to express his love for them, reassuring them that their connection would continue long after his body was gone. Although he had just completed his fourth book and was about to go on a book tour to promote it, his cancer made that impossible. Despite his disappointment, Bob said, "I'm proud of the contribution I've made." Bob wanted to experience his last days as consciously as he did his life, and so he refused all but the minimal dosage of pain medication. His was a beautiful and peaceful transition.

Not everyone is given the time to plan and reflect on one's last days or exit strategy, but we can choose to gratefully and mindfully live each day as though it were our last.

Celebrate Me Home

The first time that I met Suzi was as a guest and amateur photographer at a festive gathering to honor, celebrate and support her. The following story is about Suzi and her friends, who made humor, love, and joy as much a part of the dying process as it was a part of her life.

"Hey, look at this fun top! It would look great on you." The energy was light and playful as the group of women discovered fabulous clothes and accessories, helping each other to put together the perfect outfit.

Lilie and her daughter, Lisa, the owners of a boutique, *Violette*, had created a celebratory atmosphere with wine, cheese, and flowers for their dear friend Suzi and fifty of her closest friends. The shopping extravaganza to raise money for Suzi's medical expenses was a chance for her to party with these friends, knowing that it might be the last time that they would be together.

Who was this remarkable person who attracted so much love and joy into her life?

I couldn't help but notice her as she walked in the door. A lovely, petite woman with closely cropped hair and bright eyes, speaking in an adorable Australian accent, Suzi was so full of life that even the oxygen tube couldn't diminish her presence. She was immediately enveloped in hugs.

Lilie remembers it as "an evening of community with everyone just loving each other and expressing their caring of Suzi, who sat in a chair and intimately received each one." Suzi was in her element, caught up in the bubbling energy around her.

Recalling a very different experience just a few days earlier, Lilie says, "I was sitting in the hospital office with Suzi when she was told that she had only one, maybe two, weeks to live. Suzi sat there with a puzzled expression on her face. As the reality set in, she looked at me and said, 'Criminy. I'm f…ed!' "

"You're going to teach us all how to die," Lilie told her, and that is exactly what Suzi did. "She didn't give up. She inspired all of us in the way that she just dwelled in each day and what she could bring to it."

Her friends and family were grateful when Suzi's life was extended for another six weeks.

"Suzi's gift was in her willingness to ask and to receive, and she was so gracious about it," says Lilie. When asked how she would like to spend her last days, Suzi was clear that she wanted her house to be decorated for the holidays, with the fireplace going, and friends laughing, partying, and having a good time.

"She had so many friends wanting to be there for her that we had to create a schedule," Lilie says. "She loved being read to and indulged with lavender lotion, bubble bath, lilies, and everything that made her feel delighted. Sometimes she would get cranky, as any of us would, but you could just look into her beautiful eyes and you would see just pure spirit and pure love. At other times she would ask, 'Just lie next to me and hold my hand.' "

At one point, the tumor in her belly was so huge that Suzi looked pregnant. She encouraged her friends to paint designs on her belly, as well as on her knees, so that she could look down and see lots of flowers and happy faces.

"Suzi was a real gift to all of us," says Lilie. "She didn't disappear into herself, but let the experience be an expression of who she was. She was willing to share her death as fully as she engaged in her life, inviting us to celebrate her transition home. It was a beautiful and seamless thing."

♡ *If you were told that you had one week to live, how would you choose to experience your last days and hours? What would you do differently?*

♡ *How can you re-create your life so that whenever it is your time, you would continue doing what brings you joy, for as long as possible?*

♡ *How can you show up for a friend or family member who is dying, so that it becomes a celebration and acknowledgement of their life?*

Out of Loss

I've never felt a pain that didn't bear a blessing.
– Gene Knudson Hoffman

Loss of any kind can leave you feeling immobilized, scared, and alone, but especially when it's the loss of a loved one. Whether through death or divorce, it can feel as though a part of you is missing. You may alternate between pain and numbness, denial, anger, and fear. There is no set time to be complete with the grieving process, no goal to work towards. In fact, the feelings can show up at any time and may never totally leave you. What can be transforming is your willingness to go into the grief and to acknowledge it, to trust that it has a message. Sometimes one must go into the fire to emerge reborn.

When Laurel Rund lost Marty, her husband and trusted friend of 42 years, she was grief-stricken. In time she began to explore "who Laurel is now," discovering a passion for art and poetry through which she could express her sorrow and honor her husband's memory. Her journey brought her a new sense of purpose and gave her an opportunity to help others to move through their grieving process with more ease. Now, whenever Laurel meets someone who has experienced a loss, she doesn't say "I'm sorry," she says "I understand."

We all have or will experience loss in our lives, but our grief doesn't have to be debilitating. Nance, a hospice volunteer, who also lost her husband, believes that loss is an opportunity to soften to one another. She says, "Death is not JUST an ending ... it´s also a beginning of something new and different."

As you will see in the following stories, out of the ashes of loss can come unexpected gifts, like a beautiful garden, growing in ways that we could never have envisioned.

Sean's Garden

Yvonne holds court wherever she happens to be: the pool, the YMCA women's locker room, or on the dance floor of Sarasota's bayside reggae club. Tiny but dynamic, she inspires people of all ages and walks of life to get involved in various fundraisers, classes, and social activities.

Behind Yvonne's broad smile is a place of sadness and loss, from which she has recently emerged to create a better life experience for others.

Three years ago, Yvonne's twenty-two-year-old son, Sean, died in his sleep. For more than a year afterward, her transparent grief provided friends an opportunity to give her their love and support. Now she's ready to give back and to share what Sean's short, but full life was all about.

Yvonne, who had been raised as a single child, had not wanted her one-year-old adopted daughter to grow up without a brother or sister. So after many prayers, she and her husband decided to adopt again.

Unbeknownst to Yvonne, the baby boy who would come to her was born to an alcoholic and drug-addicted mother. When Sean was brought home by his adoptive parents, he was less than twenty-three hours old and was already going through withdrawal.

Yvonne noticed that her son was functionally very different from her daughter. Within the first few months, she learned of the special needs caused by fetal alcohol syndrome: Sean was developmentally disabled and had mild cerebral palsy.

Subconsciously, Yvonne may have identified with this vulnerable child, who, like her, was born to alcoholic parents. She and her husband committed to parenting Sean, but as their son got older, the challenges became greater. Eventually, it took its toll on the marriage, which ended in divorce. Yvonne decided to raise Sean on her own.

"As he was growing up, Sean was aware that he was different," said Yvonne. "He knew that he had disabilities, but that never stopped him from doing everything in his power to help others."

The greatest thrill came when he was eighteen: Sean gave part of his college money to the YMCA to create a scholarship fund. It allowed several disabled students at the local high school to attend the health club, including a wheelchair-bound classmate.

Jim Purdy, the Executive Vice President of the Sarasota County YMCA, says, "There were so many things stacked against this young man and yet, he was able to set up a foundation to help children in need. Sean held three jobs at one time, and he always had a kind word for people. That's pretty good in my book."

Each week Sean would set aside a part of his paycheck to add monies to this fund. With extra cash in his pocket, he could hardly wait to spend it helping others. "Mom, give $10 to that person" (who looked down and out), or "That man looks hungry. Let's buy him dinner."

Sean was a gentle soul with a unique disposition who, at twenty years of age, was only reading at a second-grade level. What made Sean special was his humanitarian spirit.

In his brief lifetime, Sean touched many lives. After his passing, his "celebration of life" was attended by almost 400 people. Jim Purdy says, "I loved Sean. He made us all better."

Members and employees of the Y, who have become like Yvonne's family, still remember what would have been Sean's birthday each year, and sign a card wishing him a "Happy Birthday in heaven." It sits on the counter behind the registration desk, amid photos of Sean from childhood through his final year.

Yvonne's desire to share the memory of her son incites her to help others. Most recently, she went on a mission to Haiti to assist with oral hygiene among orphans. Yvonne put a request out to friends, and in a short time, she collected more than 400 toothbrushes, floss, and tubes of toothpaste.

"While it's a privilege to go on these humanitarian trips to Third World countries, the needs are great in our own backyard. The avenue we travel each day is where we need to be. That's what motivates me," she says. In fact, you can't get into Yvonne's car without being enveloped by clothing and canned goods, which she's earmarked for delivery to any number of local shelters and half way houses.

"Sean was my inspiration and taught me to see things in people that I never saw before, and that gift continues," says Yvonne. "I miss the companionship of his loving and open spirit, but I'm able to see his presence in each person who shows up in my life."

In Sean's honor, his mom planted a garden with an array of colorful flowers and two pairs of his shoes, now inhabited by cactus plants. *Sean's Garden* is flourishing as it welcomes members and visitors to the YMCA. It's just one of the many ways that his memory lives on.

♡ *Have you ever experienced a loss and been unable to function?*

♡ *How were others able to show up for you to ease your pain?*

♡ *Have you been able to do that for someone else?*

Cookie's Kids

Cookie has always loved kids. As a young girl, she took on the responsibility of helping to raise her four siblings, and she said, "I could hardly wait to have a family of my own someday."

Years later, she was thrilled to finally have that chance. But as her difficult pregnancy was nearing its completion, the complications became insurmountable. Despite the best efforts of the hospital staff, baby Hope died just a few days after her birth. Cookie found comfort in being able to hold her daughter, but was overwhelmed with feelings of loss. The pain became more poignant when she was told that she could never get pregnant again.

She started to bargain with God: "If you let me have another child, I will devote my life to children." Two years later, Cookie gave birth to a son.

And she never forgot her promise. Shortly after Timmy was born, Cookie started volunteering as a teacher's aid. Later, she met a young woman who was a foster mom, and thought, *That's a way I could honor my bargain.* She got approval to have a foster home.

It was the beginning of a six-and-a-half-year commitment to foster children — and sometimes their teenage moms. "They were my family, my kids," she says of the more than 100 children who lived with her for anywhere from a few months to several years. One young boy, who, at two years old was severely neglected and abused, lived with Cookie for two years before he was adopted.

Recently, just after his eighteenth birthday, his adoptive parents took him to visit Cookie, whom he calls his "Rainbow Mom."

Cookie learned a lot about flexibility when she adopted Roxanne, a four-year-old girl born to an alcoholic mother. The teenage years were especially rough when the addictions, hormones and attachment disorders took over, but Cookie's love and perseverance paid off. Her daughter is now 22 and wants to become a therapist.

Currently, Cookie is a paraprofessional in child-protection services, where she brings hope to homes and families where there is none. She believes that most of the time parents weren't parented themselves, and they don't know how to do it for their own children. "When they can see what unconditional love looks like, they learn how to love themselves and then their families," says Cookie. She especially loves working with those whom others find challenging: very young parents and those who are developmentally disabled. "It takes being flexible and thinking outside of the box."

She believes "life is like a ripple in the pond—everything you do touches someone's life. I may not like the choices that people make, but I can help someone to make different choices." Cookie's goal is that no parent should feel like they don't know how to love their children. She tells the parents: "If you can find joy in your child even when they're testing you to the limits, then I've done my job." And she works hard to make sure that no children feel like they don't have a loving, healthy adult in their lives.

"I am truly blessed," says Cookie. "It took going through my 'dark night of the soul' to find my purpose. If Hope had survived, I would have never taken this path."

And that path has itself brought tremendous hope and love to many people.

♡ *Have you ever suffered a loss that felt debilitating and incomprehensible?*

♡ *Is there a message that you can you share with others about how to transcend loss and create a new level of hope?*

♡ *Have you ever bargained with God for something you desperately wanted or needed?*

♡ *What was the result?*

Six
Kids and Kritters

There's a kid in all of us.
– YMCA logo for the Strong Kids Campaign

You may be wondering how children and animals ended up in the same chapter. *What are the similarities?* you might ask, a question that I, too, have pondered.

For me, there's an innocence, vulnerability and a sweetness in animals and children before they've been conditioned and trained by adults. They are uniquely themselves and express their feelings spontaneously and naturally. There seems to be an alliance of energies, and an inquisitive and fresh approach to everything around them.

Kids and critters have a natural intuitive sense about who they can trust, who they can be open with. They seem to know when someone is sad or hurt and they try to make it better, whether with licks or hugs.

When children are playing together, before they've been taught to notice differences in each other, they are caught up in the moment of just having fun. Like kids, young animals are free spirited, playful, and curious. Actually, these qualities are in all of us when we stop living our life so carefully, editing and screening everything we do and say.

I loved the photos posted on the Internet, and shared in emails, of the animals that were rescued in the aftermath of Hurricane

Katrina. Different breeds and species of animals in a variety of sizes and shapes were put into the back seat of a car, all jumbled together.

Whenever a newcomer was added, the animals shifted around and within minutes, cats, dogs, and other critters were all cuddled together, grateful to be out of the storm. It was a heartening image. For me, it validates that love is our natural state, which is readily apparent when we are all in the "same boat," so to speak.

Here's an Oscar's nod to the stories in this chapter, acknowledging one very special kid, a one-of-kind dog, as well as a compassionate veterinarian who found value in the love that two little girls had for their puppy.

Kids Who Care

Every child comes with the message
that God is not yet discouraged of man.
— Rabindranath Tagore

Whenever I meet children who are kind, confident, and engaged in life, who communicate and connect with others, I'm appreciative of the parents and guardians who inspire and impart such values. It's the younger generation who offers hope for a peaceable and unified world.

Walking on the Boulder mall one sunny afternoon, I was drawn to the upbeat sounds of a fiddle. A young boy was playing lively Celtic tunes to raise money for, and awareness of, the plight of dolphins in Japan. Near a bookstore, he'd set up a handmade sign and propped open his fiddle case, which was quickly filling up with dollar bills dropped by passersby. I spoke to eleven-year-old Hayden during a break in the music. He asked me if I'd seen the video about the slaughtering of the dolphins, and when

I responded that I hadn't, he gave me the website link. I was touched by his determination to make a difference in the world, not only through his fund-raising efforts, but by other volunteer activities, which he mentioned he's involved in.

I dropped a dollar into his case and walked into the bookstore. When I came out several minutes later, I saw another fiddle player in the spot Haiden had vacated. Intrigued, I walked up to him, and was surprised to learn that he was Haiden's eight-year-old brother. His sign requested donations for the education of young girls in China because, he said, "I'm Chinese, you know."

It created an unforgettable impression. I was awed by these boys, who stood up for causes they believed in, and by their parents who nurtured and sustained such altruistic qualities.

One Step at a Time

> *Climb every mountain ... 'til you find your dream.*
> –Richard Rodgers, *The Sound of Music*

It's especially heartening to encounter kids helping other kids, supporting and celebrating their successes as much as they would their own, and being a good friend. It's what led me to follow up on a story that I had read in Boulder's local newspaper.

I met ten-year-old Matt Moniz and his dad, Mike, at an indoor climbing wall, where we'd scheduled an appointment for an interview. Like a typical kid, Matt was easily distracted by the movements and noise of the other climbers, but he politely answered questions about what he had accomplished in his life and what his goals were.

Matt's story is an inspiring example of what's possible when parents enable their children to follow their dreams. In doing so, these kids change not only the lives of those they meet, but also their own.

Matt Moniz, who recently started middle school in Boulder, Colorado, has already seen and experienced more than most people will in a lifetime. At ten years old, Matt set the world's record as the youngest person to summit Cerro Aconcagua in Argentina, the highest mountain in the Americas, with a daunting elevation of 22,841 feet.

Along with his dad, he has climbed two of the Seven Summits, the highest mountains on all seven continents: Mount Kilimanjaro, the tallest peak in Africa, and Russia's Elbrus, the uppermost point in Europe. "It's not about breaking records," Matt says. "It's about experiencing the mountains and the culture of the people who live in these countries."

His passion started when he, his twin sister Kaylee, and their parents visited the Khumbu Valley in Nepal to stay at the Everest base camp. They learned that the village was in need of computers and a new school building. Matt realized that he could best help people in the village by raising money, which is exactly what he did, and he hasn't stopped since. Every major trip that Matt has taken involves a community service project.

Matt's biggest motivation for climbing in the last year has been to support his best friend, nine-year-old Ian, who, at age six, was diagnosed with PAH (Pulmonary Arterial Hypertension). It's a rare disease, affecting about one in a million people, and not often seen in someone so young.

When Matt and Ian, who have played together most of their lives, were running up the road recently, Matt was shocked to realize that, after just fifteen steps, Ian was panting hard. "What Ian was going through was what I experience at the top of the highest summits, except that Ian feels that every day," explains Matt. "The symptoms are a lot like pulmonary edema that mountain climbers can get—headaches and feelings of being dizzy, tired, and confused."

Matt had an idea to raise money for his friend's medical expenses, only part of which was covered by insurance. He set a goal of climbing fourteen "14ers" in fourteen days to create awareness of PAH. Since Colorado has the most 14,000-plus-foot peaks in the country, he could accomplish his goal in his own back yard. Not only did "Team Moniz" (including Matt, his dad, and Ian's dad) climb fourteen peaks, they did it in only eight days, and raised more than $20,000 from donations and corporate sponsors.

The publicity that Matt received has made him a celebrity, although he quietly brings the focus back to the main reason that he did it: to help his best friend. In fact, Matt says that on the toughest day, when he wanted to quit the whole thing, he saw a picture of Ian's face in his mind. That was all it took to keep going. "The toughest parts of the climb were like walking in Ian's shoes."

After every major trip, Matt and Ian have a sleepover. "We play a bunch of games, and I show pictures and tell him a bunch of stories," says Matt.

When Matt and Kaylee recently celebrated their birthday, they asked for money, rather than presents. With the $600 they collected, they personally traveled to the Amani Children's Home for Street Orphans in Tanzania. The orphans, many of them abandoned by their families, had sores, were without shoes, and several had contracted AIDS. "The kids hugged us, and that felt weird at first, but then it felt good," says Matt. "We're glad to give them money for food, clothes, and books."

Mike is proud of both of his children, who love the chance to not only contribute, but to learn about other world cultures. Matt enjoyed teaching English to a group of Massai children on one of his trips. Kaylee, who is hearing impaired, is planning a service project of her own: donating hearing aids to an orphanage in New Guinea.

"American children have a lot," says Mike. "I'm glad that Matt and Kaylee have the opportunity to see people with very little material possessions, yet who feel blessed and happy."

Mike Moniz finds it "indescribable to travel the world with my son." He believes that every mountain experience turns you into a better person. "There's a personal transformation that occurs when you confront seemingly insurmountable challenges, both those that are external and those in your mind," he says.

Through these invaluable life lessons, Matt is already demonstrating confidence, caring, and awareness. When asked, "What would you do if you had one wish and could use it for anything that you wanted," he thinks for a while before responding, "*Anything* in the whole world?...Then, I would cure everyone of PAH."

His dad smiles.

Since this interview, Matt has been named "Ambassador for the Outdoor Industry Foundation," with a mission of inspiring children to get outdoors. He and his dad spent one summer breaking the speed record for High Pointers: They climbed fifty of the tallest peaks, including Alaska's Denali, in all fifty states in forty-three days, three hours, and fifty-one minutes. And the latest record breaking news is that Matt has the distinction of being named the youngest "National Geographic Adventurer of the Year"!

The plan now is to relax and enjoy normal everyday activities. In fact, Matt blends in so well that his teachers and fellow students are often unaware of his amazing accomplishments. To Matt, it's all just a part of life.

♡ *In what ways can you help young people to see the possibilities in their lives and inspire altruistic visions and behavior?*

♡ *What have you learned or experienced that you would like to share with these children?*

♡ *And what are you learning from the kids in your world about making a difference?*

Bag Full of Small Change

*Any glimpse into the life of an animal quickens our own
and makes it so much the larger and better in every way.*

– John Muir

For many years, C.T. Mills felt privileged to work with her father, a well-loved veterinarian in a small New England town. In her own words, she shares the following story about an ordinary morning in an extraordinary man's day:

Doctor Mills, or "Doc," as most people call him, has the wonderful ability to see the good in everyone and everything. His philosophy is that the health and well-being of animals is his primary goal; money is secondary.

During office hours one morning, I opened the waiting room door to find two young girls sitting on the bench, neither of whom I recognized. One had a rather corpulent Chihuahua on her lap, and the other clutched a clear plastic bag full of small change. A taxi waited outside, its meter running.

"Can I help you?" I asked politely, hoping that a grownup with a wallet would appear.

The older girl, barely making eye contact, answered in broken English, "Juanita," pointing to the well-fed Chihuahua squirming in her lap, "She needs shots. How much?" The younger girl, after a nudge from her sister, pushed the plastic bag, bulging with pennies, nickels, and dimes in my direction.

I scurried through the office door looking for Doc. He was in the pharmacy filling prescriptions. Leaning close, I whispered, "There are two girls with a dog that needs her vaccinations."

Peering over his bifocals, he replied, "So let them in. And why are you whispering?"

"Because all they have is a plastic bag of small change. And I am pretty sure there's not enough to cover the office call and vaccines." I continued to whisper, "Tons of P-E-N-N-I-E-S. Get my drift?"

Doc smiled and whispered back, "Let them in."

Juanita promptly received her exam and vaccines. As Doc filled out a certificate, the older girl spoke up, "How much?" Promptly, the little one dangled the bag of change toward him.

"Well ... whatever is in the bag," he said decisively, trading the plastic bag for Juanita's vaccination certificate. Smiling, he handed it to me, winked, then whispered, "Count this when you have time."

I watched the girls, holding Juanita, get in the taxi before turning to Doc. "I'll bet you a root beer float there's not enough money, not even close."

"It doesn't matter," he said. "What does matter is they care about their dog. That'll make up the difference."

As was so often the case, I learned a valuable life lesson from Dad that morning: Money is not always the only means of payment.

♡ *Have you even used a currency other than money to purchase a service or product?*

♡ *In what ways have you contributed, or would you be willing to contribute, your skill or talent to help someone without the means to pay you?*

♡ *What would it feel like to give or to receive without counting?*

Kritters and Kindness

I think I could turn and live with animals.
They do not sweat and whine about their condition.
Not one is dissatisfied.

— Walt Whitman

As I sipped my birthday margarita at a local tiki bar by the Sarasota Bay, I noticed a three-legged, reddish pit bull, not far from where I sat.

Unable to resist, I walked over to this fetching dog, whose

"smile" extended from one pointed ear to the other. Following the leash to the person holding it, I met Tom Hudson, who formally introduced me to Pippi. I discovered that not only is she the sweetest pit bull I've ever met, but she's a celebrity of sorts in Tom's law practice and at a local rehab hospital.

Although *Love Is the New Currency* is about two-legged beings, it is impossible to exclude the animal kingdom, especially the critters who intimately share our homes and lives. Pippi represents the numerous loyal and loving animals who bring gifts of love, joy, and comfort to our world.

Following is Pippi's story, as told by Tom.

Pippi the Pitbull

My wife Ruth and I first heard about a red nose pit bull named Pippi when Dr. Laurie, a veterinarian at our local animal clinic, asked us if we wanted another dog. We already had two dogs: a black Lab mix named Lucky and a pit bull-boxer mix named Rosie. Dr. Laurie insisted that Pippi was a great dog, even if she wasn't in good shape—her ears were all torn up and she had a nasty gash across her throat, but worst of all, her right shoulder was dislocated. From her condition and the part of town where she was found, it appeared that she was a victim of the odious practice of dog fighting. Because of the delay in getting medical treatment, her leg could not be saved.

At first we thought it was out of the question. *A third dog? How could we do it?* But after declining to adopt Pippi, our daughter, Sarah, urged us to give this dog a chance and to save her from possible euthanization. We went back and saw her again. Nobody could say "no" to Pippi twice. So we didn't. She came home with us and became part of our family.

Pippi was with us for over a year before we realized that wherever we went, it was always Pippi that everyone noticed and remembered.

When my mother was ill and was recovering for a week at a

rehabilitation hospital, the staff encouraged family members to bring pets to visit. Those who met Pippi would frequently remark that she would lift the spirits of someone who had just lost a limb. After all, nobody knows better than Pippi how much a catastrophic injury can change the rest of one's life.

Towards the end of that week, one of the nurses approached me and asked, "What would you think about Pippi becoming a volunteer dog to cheer up the patients?" I thought about it for a moment, envisioning the strain of running my business. "I don't know," I said. "I'm pretty busy these days."

The nurse smiled and said, "I didn't say we needed *you*." Having been brought down a peg, I thought about it, and decided that Pippi is a gift who should be shared. So now, Pippi has begun a new chapter. She is a volunteer at the rehabilitation hospital, visiting the patients every weekend. And you should see how a visit from Pippi puts a smile on the patients' faces.

On one visit, just as we were about to leave the hospital, an older couple came up to us and asked if we had been to the room of their son, who had recently lost his leg in a motorcycle accident. I decided that Pippi and I needed to visit this young man.

At the doorway, I noticed the man's head turned toward the back wall, and asked the question that I usually do: "Does anyone in here like dogs?" No answer, but I decided to walk in anyway.

The young man turned and looked at us and asked, "Does that dog have only three legs?"

In the meantime, Pippi had gone over to the corner of the room, where there was a full prosthetic leg and hip, and barked at it. The man laughed. Looking at Pippi, he said, "Looks like we're in the same club!"

He asked for Pippi to come up on the bed with him, and as Pippi started licking his face, he started crying. The young man petted her for twenty minutes, crying as he held her.

When we got home, I shared the experience with my wife Ruth, who commented on Pippi's courageous, can-do-it spirit. "The only one who doesn't know that she's missing a leg is Pippi. That attitude never fails to inspire others."

At a recent luncheon to honor the volunteers at the hospital, Tom arrived alone and the staff asked, "Where's Pippi?" Tom replied "I didn't realize I was supposed to bring her to the luncheon." At their request, he went back home to get Pippi, but rather than feeling upstaged, Tom beamed with pride at his sweet dog who brings joy wherever she goes.

♡ *Do you have a pet that provides comfort and companionship?*

♡ *Does your pet know when you or others are sad or not feeling well?*

♡ *How does he/she offer affection and love?*

♡ *Are there ways that you can share your pet with others?*

Seven
Life Savers

Life is either a daring adventure,
or nothing.
— Helen Keller

L ife is precious. We witness and celebrate the birth of a baby as a miracle, despite the fact that these miracles have been taking place for many thousands of years.

The very act of breathing is something we often take for granted, even though it's our life force, and without it we wouldn't exist. Have you ever lost your breath for a few seconds, whether through choking or taking in too much water? It's a frightening moment when you gasp for air and realize that nothing is more important than simply taking another breath.

And when we are aware that our next breath, or that of someone we love, could be the last, we value that gift of life and usually wish for a little more time. We realize how quickly life can be cut short. We're not indestructible, and there's no warranty on how long our body will last. While many believe "when it's your time, it's your time," we never truly know when that is. But sometimes, just when we think our life is over, someone or something intercedes and buys us a little more time.

This chapter is about life savers—individuals who seize opportunities to give others the gift of more time. Whether through the donation of organs, the courageous confronting of nature in crisis, or the prevention of a violent act, the following stories acknowledge the bravery of individuals who played a role in keeping death at bay.

To the Rescue

I've often wondered what it is that makes some people willing to sacrifice their own life to save that of another? Is there a point at which they weigh the potential consequences of an act and decide to take a chance, knowing that there may not be a second one? Or are some people simply wired to help, their altruistic actions so innate that they respond automatically, like a knee-jerk reaction, with no thought of the outcome?

Faced with a life or death situation, sometimes there is little or no time to think about what to do, there is only a narrow window of opportunity to act quickly in order to give someone else a chance to live … even at the risk of cutting short one's own.

Many of us who watched or read the news story of the Queensland flooding in Australia were deeply touched by the decision of thirteen-year-old Jordan Rice, who sacrificed his own life to save his ten-year-old brother Blake. Despite a fear of water, Jordan begged a passerby who was trying to help: "Save my brother." Once Blake was safe, Jordan said, "Please save my mum." But he and his mother were swept away by the current and drowned. On Twitter, Jordan was dubbed "the true hero" of the Queensland floods.

Here are two stories of everyday heroes, for whom saving lives is just a natural part of who they are and what they do. Thanks to their courage and instincts, several people have been able to experience one more day.

Appreciating Life

David Camacho, the buff, fifty-two-year-old owner of a popular bodybuilding gym in Gilroy, California, was working out with a client and telling him about a recent robbery in town. Jose and Trinidad, a couple in their sixties, were held up two weeks before, right in front of the local bank. Someone apparently knew that they cashed substantial checks from their business every Friday, and Jose, with cash in his hand, was stabbed just outside the front door.

The couple, along with their children, ran a little food market directly across the street from David's gym, although he didn't shop there. He was aware that there had been a rash of local robberies, and that the police had been unable to catch the robbers.

Just minutes after he finished telling the story, David was standing by the front door with his client, taking a short break, when he witnessed a rapidly unfolding scene across the street. "You won't believe this," he said. "They're going to be robbed again!"

Jose, Trinidad, and their son, Nicando, were about to enter their store when a blue sedan pulled up. The driver jumped out holding a shotgun, which he pointed at Jose's face, while a passenger and a man in the back seat remained in the car.

David knew from experience that a pump shotgun had a manual slide and would take a few seconds to work. Bolting through the open door, and yelling loudly, he ran as fast as he could toward the man holding the shotgun. "The guy pointed it at me," says David, "but I was screaming and running hard at him, and in confusion, he jumped in the car and sped off."

A week later, the robbers were apprehended. For his part, David was given "The Good Egg" award by the Gilroy Chamber of Commerce. Overnight, his reputation shifted from jock to courageous hero, although he was surprised to be singled out.

"Anyone would do the same thing if given the chance," he says.

When asked if he had experienced any fear, he says, "You don't think about it, you just jump in and help. I've saved the lives of others a bunch of times." One instance he recalls involved a police officer who was being held down and beaten by an ex-con. No one was stepping in to help. David had noticed that the ex-con had his gun unwrapped, and definitely had the upper hand. "I just jumped on both of them, which allowed the police officer to regain his position and save himself."

David says, "I've always been for the underdog." That often got him in trouble as he was growing up. "I've almost been killed numerous times—from stabbings, and once when I tried to prevent the robbery of my van. I flirted with death a lot in the early days."

David wasn't considered a good student. He says, "My self-esteem was in the toilet. I never felt I was good enough." But he later discovered that he excelled in one arena: bodybuilding. As a competitive bodybuilder, his titles included Mr. Texas and Mr. Sacramento. Bodybuilding got him away from his hometown and earned him accolades and recognition. Life was good, and he was loving it.

One day, when David was in his early thirties, he was enjoying a rare afternoon fishing with his younger brother, Mike. David was accustomed to flat-bottom fishing boats, but not the angle and movements of their canoe. As he tried to walk across it, it capsized, sending both brothers into the frigid water. The shore was 100 yards away, and the fiberglass canoe had already drifted about 90 feet away. Neither of them could swim.

I'm drowning, David realized, as his lungs filled up with water and the weight of his heavy shoes and jacket made him sink. He had an out-of-body experience in which he could see himself go down and thought: *I can't believe it. I'm not going to make it.* He looked over at his brother, whom he loved, and was sad that he couldn't save him or himself.

Suddenly, he heard a voice: "Remember all the times you tried to end your life? Just relax now." David started to let go, but something made him resist. *No. I've got more to do!* He fought to get back up to the surface and was overwhelmed with joy to see that the canoe had drifted sideways toward them. "I started bawling like a baby when I realized that we would be saved," says David. "My brother and I each held on to an end of the canoe and then side-kicked to shore. Once safely on land, we looked over to where we had almost drowned and there was a beautiful rainbow reflected on the water."

From that point on, David's life seemed to take many positive turns, supporting his belief that things happen for a good reason. Eventually, he ended up back in his hometown, where serendipity led him to open his own bodybuilding gym.

While he's surrounded by huge photos of himself and plaques for the many competitive bodybuilding awards he's won, he says, "I don't want to be that guy anymore. I get far more satisfaction supporting someone else's rise to success."

David focuses on helping others, especially the young boys who are drawn to his gym. He teaches them bodybuilding, and shares another of his passions, archery, for which he once earned an Olympic bronze medal as a member of Team USA.

He has mentored one young boy for ten years and has just taken on another, a fourteen-year-old who, when he was younger, would walk by David's gym, longing to work out there but unable to afford a membership. David is happy to give him that opportunity because he knows that by offering him an alternative to the gang activities that he's been involved in, the teen stands a good chance of changing his life. David finds it a wonderful way to give back.

As for Jose, Trinidad, and their offspring, they have made David an honorary member of their family, inviting him to important occasions, where he is welcomed and repeatedly thanked for saving Jose's life.

Now at the most peaceful place in his life, David says: "I like myself, and the more I like myself, the more I can help others."

♡ *What would you have done if you were David and witnessed such a harrowing scene?*

♡ *What, if anything, would motivate you to risk your own life to save another's?*

♡ *What would you be willing to do to give someone a chance to change the direction of their life?*

On-Call Hero

Calm, confident, and solid in both stature and character, A.J. Hotchkiss is the kind of man to whom you could entrust your life, and in fact, many people have done just that. A.J. got an early start as a hero when he was nine years old. He was home alone with his mom when she went into shock and passed out. A.J. remained calm, doing everything he had learned through his Cub Scout training while he waited for a doctor to respond to his emergency call. A.J. was later credited with saving his mother's life.

When A.J. was a teen, he was allowed to ride around New York with his grandfather, a long-time fire chief, who investigated arson cases. Little did he realize that he would one day have an opportunity to fill those big boots.

Decades later, A.J. moved with his wife, Lenore, to a sparsely populated Colorado mountain community (about one family per forty acres.) The town's 23,000 residents were totally dependent on a volunteer fire department. Despite the demands of their growing real estate business, A.J. contributed eleven years to the department, five of those as fire chief.

Under A.J.'s command, two fire stations were designed and built with updated equipment, one of which was later dedicated as the "A.J. Hotchkiss Fire Station." It wasn't long before these stations were put to the test in a major way.

Two days after A.J. retired, he was called in to take command of the Cedar Mountain fire, a huge fire caused by lightning. Despite the volatile conditions that threatened his community, within two hours A.J. had brought together a volunteer force of eighty-four people. In three long, hard days, they successfully stopped what would have been a major catastrophe.

Two months later, the Hayman Fire, which was known, at the time, as the biggest fire in Colorado's history, started just a few miles away when a Park Service employee carelessly burned a "Dear Jane" letter, despite the extremely high wild fire risk.

Because of incompatible radio frequencies, poor communication, and incorrect information given to Forward Intelligence, the fire, which had started in nearby Park County, was greatly underestimated. The initial call went out to only a five-man crew. Since the fire started on federal property, A.J., who was a director of the Fire Board, wasn't authorized to respond until it crossed his county's lines. That didn't happen for three days and by then the fire was raging out of control.

With 1,800 people in the line of the fire, A.J., his group of volunteers, and the sheriff responded immediately, evacuating everyone safely. That wasn't an easy task in an area that, because of its mountainous terrain, had no cell phone or television reception. Only after the area was vacated could they turn their full attention to fighting the fire.

"I spent fifteen hours a day of the hardest fifteen days that I've ever spent in my life fighting that fire," A.J. says. There were eleven firefighters, victims of the forced evacuations, bunking down in the Hotchkiss' home, along with numerous volunteers exhaustedly working on the front lines, and evacuees, all needing to be fed (amounting to 120 meals a day) and given water. Supported initially by an auxiliary team headed by his wife, Lenore, A.J. says, "We quickly ran out of food, water, diesel fuel, gas, and money. We begged and borrowed money for what we needed and our community responded."

There were brief moments of humor throughout the ordeal. "Evacuating people with such short notice meant that most of them couldn't get their livestock out," says A.J. "Wranglers were called in, which became a logistical nightmare. Real cowboys, yelling 'Yee haw!' didn't have much experience wrangling a thousand-pound pig! There was also one independent-minded mule that got loose and ran alongside the fire trucks, but no one could catch him."

By the fifteenth day, the fire had already destroyed 113,000 acres of land. "It was unimaginable to be in the midst of a fire that size," says A.J. There was no time to be afraid. His group, working tirelessly, was instrumental in keeping the fire at bay along a six-mile fire line. None of the homes in their area were lost.

After a lifetime of saving others, A.J. came close to losing his own life three years ago after suffering a heart attack and before undergoing triple bi-pass surgery. He told Lenore, his wife of thirty years, "I'm going."

Fortunately, A.J. survived. "I've performed CPR many times and never thought I'd be on the receiving end. I died and even got to experience the tunnel and the light before being revived." Upon his return, the first thing he said was, "I'm back. Now how do I get out of here?"

A.J. says the near-death experience gave him a whole new perspective on life. "Once you grasp your own mortality, it's hard to look at other people in the same way. I now have a more relaxed, less critical, and more forgiving attitude toward others. After all, we're all in this life together—we're all born and we all die."

Since then, A.J. has found a new way to contribute to his rural community. His early experiences with Internet communication were the inspiration for creating an online radio station called *The Voice of Teller County*. "Since most people don't have very good radio signals here, it's the perfect solution," says A.J. "There's not another system like it."

He's also created a sophisticated emergency-notification system that includes enhanced 911 services. Teller County will be the first to try out the new system, which will allow 6,000 calls a minute. Fire notification will be the top priority. "It's critical to keep people informed," A.J. says. "If communication can save lives, and I believe it can, then that's what we'll be doing."

♡ *Have you ever been in a life-threatening situation or had a near-death experience?*

♡ *What thoughts were going through your mind when survival seemed only a remote possibility?*

♡ *Did the experience give you a new perspective on your life? How?*

♡ *Would you be willing to confront a wild fire to save lives?*

Donors

You often say, "I would give, but only to the deserving."
The trees in your orchard say not so, nor the flocks in your pastures.
They give that they may live, for to withhold is to perish.
– Kahlil Gibran

Would you give up one of your kidneys to a family member if they were at risk of dying without one? What about to a friend? What if you learned that you were a perfect donor for a stranger who needed a part of your lungs to survive?

These are hard questions for most of us to answer. When I've asked that question of others, I've received varied responses. Almost always, the answer was "yes" when the donation was to save the life of a family member or a good friend. The inquiry often elicited a longer pause or sometimes a quick "no" when the donation was for a stranger. And yet, from others, I have received an unequivocal "yes"—this individual would do whatever it took to help anyone in need, even someone that they didn't know.

Several years ago, I took a class based on the book *The Tibetan Approach to Living and Dying*. Our guest speaker was Carol, a lovely woman in her forties, who shared with us what it was like to live each day aware that it could be her last. Carol had had a lung transplant a few years prior, but the lung was no longer functioning well, and she was once again on a donor list. Along with her oxygen tank, she carried a beeper to alert her if a lung became available for her. For the next several months, five of us decided to form a support team for Carol, each spending a few hours with her one day a week while her husband was at work. During that time, I learned a lot about living consciously and appreciating the present moment. Carol, unfortunately, did not receive a second chance. No one died with the compatible lung that Carole needed and she didn't survive. The experience made me realize the importance of being an organ donor when I die, to give another person a chance to live longer.

But for someone who has always been squeamish about needles, doctors, and hospitals, I can't imagine anything more difficult to give up than a part of my body while I'm in still good health, especially knowing that what I give away cannot be replaced or replenished. Yet, what could be a greater gift than giving someone the gift of life, an extension of time with loved ones, an opportunity to fulfill a need, or to leave a legacy?

Following are two stories of individuals who, when faced with such a decision, made what they felt was the only obvious choice.

Big-Deal Donor

Janet James shares her experience and reaction upon receiving an unusual request from her sibling:

A cold chill ran through my body as I read the line, "This is the hardest letter I have ever written." My stomach dropped with fear as I read the next line: "I need your kidney." My brother, Jim, got the same letter from our sister Susan. Two weeks later, I was in San Francisco and he was in Philadelphia being tested to see whose chemistry would match Susan's. One of us was going to give up a kidney for our sister, and paired with apprehension came a surprising and intense desire that I would be the one.

I got my wish: It was me who matched. The transplant occurred on November fourth. After six weeks, I returned to work, my fitness schedule, and all other normal activities. In the years that ensued I took up biking, skiing, and running. My career soared, and I raised a healthy and happy child. I literally forgot that I had only one kidney. It was a non-issue.

When people discovered I was a kidney donor, the reaction was almost always a startling sort of awe. They'd comment, "How nice you are," "How brave," or "What an amazing gift you gave." I hope I'm a nice person and I try to be brave, but when it comes to giving a kidney in exchange for a life, I am the one who received a gift.

Susan is my big sister and my role model. Growing up, she was my bedroom mate, who I kept awake at night with endless chatter, and the person with whom I shared my secrets, giggled, and cried when tragedy struck. In my eyes, she could do no wrong and I wanted to be like her, to measure up to her perfection. By giving her my kidney, I got to keep her a while longer.

Last week we celebrated our twenty-fifth transplant anniversary. Susan called it a "Celebration of Life." She organized a fund-raiser for the Restoring Hope Transplant House in Middleton, Wisconsin. The day wasn't about her, but about others, the theme of her life since the transplant.

At the event, people stood in line to thank me for Susan, for someone so special — the word I heard over and over — who had made a difference in so many lives with her genuine contributions to our larger world, her immediate circle, and many individuals on a personal basis.

I took my forty-year-old son to the event. Here is a message he sent to me the morning after we returned:

"Not exactly sure why, but the trip has changed me—I just feel more comfortable with life overall. I imagine that being with Aunt Susan and seeing all the spectacular things she does is an extreme motivator in becoming a better person. All the challenges she is faced with on a daily basis and she still has everyone else's best interests in mind and seems to take everything with a positive attitude. I know that if I just took a few extra breaths and looked more at the larger picture I could make a difference. Aunt Susan is a huge inspiration. In our short visit, it really hit home that life isn't just about the here and now, what you have and what you need, but the overall of making a difference with everyone we come into contact."

Being a donor wasn't the big deal. The big deal was the life that went on to make a difference in so many lives. Susan is still my big sister, my role model, and my inspiration. Maybe you've seen the bumper sticker: "Don't take your organs to heaven ... heaven knows we need them here!" People like Susan are the reason why.

Extending a Life

In a quaint, traditional New England fishing village, Mary Lou's curiosity was piqued by an article in her local newspaper. The second time she read the story, she couldn't stop thinking about Jim, a twenty-five-year-old with cystic fibrosis, who was going to die unless a compatible donor was willing to give him a part of their lung. He had already lost a sister to the same disease two years earlier, and no one in his family proved to be a match. Jim was asking for help to extend his time with his wife and parents. Mary Lou thought, *It would be wonderful to be able to do something like this.*

So, she offered to be tested, only to learn that someone else had already come forward. When she found out a short time later that this donor had changed his mind, she made the call to Jim's mom, assuring her: "If I'm a compatible donor for your son, I will go through with this."

At 43 years of age, physically fit and a nonsmoker, Mary Lou tested as a perfect donor. Although most of her family, and especially her dad, thought she was crazy to become a donor, to Mary Lou it felt like the most natural thing to do. "I've been fortunate in my health and here's a young guy who was dealt a bad hand. It made me realize how fragile life is and how fortunate any of us are who are blessed with good health." As a dedicated nurse who has always loved being a caretaker, she added: "I get a lot of happiness from seeing those around me happy."

On the day of the scheduled surgery, Mary Lou said she had expected to feel nervous, but instead felt peaceful. Although the surgery had to be put off a few days, creating angst for the family, Mary Lou remained calm, knowing that it would just be a matter of time. The subsequent three-hour surgery and a full month of recovery time were eased by Mary Lou's attitude, exercise regimen, and sense of well-being throughout the experience.

"I got as much out of it as he did," said Mary Lou. "I've never had children, but the first time that Jim breathed on his own it felt like my own child. He had a part of me in him."

Mary Lou discovered that she now had a whole new extended family. It included not only Mary Lou, but also her dad, who had become a regular visitor while Jim was in the hospital, where he and Jim formed a lasting bond.

Because of Mary Lou, Jim was able to enjoy another two-and-a-half years with his loved ones. On the very same day that Jim passed away Mary Lou's dad died of cancer; side-by-side photos of them appeared in the obituary section of their small-town newspaper.

Even though she lost Jim, Mary Lou was grateful to have been able to make a difference between life and death, even if for a short time. She says, "I would do it again in a heartbeat."

♡ *What would you do if your organ was a perfect match and could save someone's life?*

♡ *Could you ask someone to donate an organ to prolong your own life or that of a loved one?*

♡ *Have you considered donating your organs when you die? If so, does your driver's license indicate that you are an organ donor?*

Eight
Planetary Partners

Wheresoever you go, go with all your heart.

              – Confucius

The magnificence of the human spirit is often most evident when there is a major global or natural catastrophe, something that is beyond our control and yet compels us to do what we can to alleviate suffering and to assist those in danger. The disaster becomes the focus of our attention. It creates a sense of urgency that takes precedence over personal concerns. It doesn't matter where a catastrophe occurs people usually want to help in whatever way they can.

Technology has made the rapid spread of information an invaluable asset in being able to connect with sometimes unlikely planetary partners to provide immediate aid. For instance, in just a few days after the Haiti quake, despite the economic hardship of people throughout the world, the Red Cross raised $8 million dollars, mostly from individual ten-dollar donations made as part of a text-messaging campaign using the words Haiti and 90999. The same useage of mobile devices has also helped in raising money for Japan's earthquake/tsunami victims.

While our first priority is taking care of people's basic needs for survival, we can also express our *currency of love* by joining others throughout the world to send loving energy and prayers of support, acknowledging our universal connection to each other.

In Port au Prince, for example, following the earthquake, groups of women, who held different religious beliefs and would not normally associate with each other, chanted and prayed together each night, creating a sense of unity and hope. Stories like this remind us that our normal political and religious differences, along with prejudices, evaporate, for the most part, when we recognize our planetary partnership and work together to aid others.

When we are willing to suspend our lives long enough to open our hearts, reach into our pocketbooks, and physically, emotionally, or energetically offer assistance to ease the pain and suffering of each other, our actions inspire hope and promise for a better world.

Comfort in Chaos

Cherish all living beings with a boundless heart,
radiating kindness over the entire world.

– Buddha

Each cataclysmic event brings awareness of just how fragile our life on Planet Earth can be, and how valuable our connection to and reliance on other human beings to offer comfort, aid, and support. Disaster can strike anywhere at any time; none of us are immune.

I learned how quickly things can shift at a young age. When I was five years old, a dam burst in the "flats," the section of town where we lived. Looking out from our third floor apartment, I watched cars floating down the street and people being lowered from their homes by ropes. I wasn't scared until my cousin, Willie, who was two years older, started crying and praying. A few hours later, we were rescued by row boat. I took the only thing that I was concerned about leaving behind—my pet rabbit.

When I was twelve, my family moved to a second floor apartment next to my dad's variety store. We had only lived there a few months when we were preparing to have a party to celebrate my youngest brother Tyler's first birthday. My mom had gone next door to work while my dad went out for something to eat. The knock at the door surprised my other brother, Bob, and me. We weren't expecting company to arrive for at least another hour.

"Get out of the house! There's a fire!" we were told by our downstairs neighbors. I grabbed my baby brother, and Bob and I ran down the stairs to safety. While the family of six, who lived below us, lost everything, thankfully, no one was hurt. We had extensive smoke damage in our apartment and chose not to move back to that home.

In both cases, we were fortunate that we were ok and that we had family members to take us in. I was amazed at how quickly our lives had changed without warning.

When I witness those who have escaped natural disasters with just the clothes on their back and nowhere to go, or worse, to have lost their homes, families and friends, I want to reach out and comfort them. This kind of response, I think, is part of our human nature. We want to help each other, to aid our planetary partners wherever they may be in whatever way we can. Even when we are the ones who have experienced loss and must find the courage and strength to carry on, we find comfort in comforting others, in expressing our compassion and unity. We know we are not alone.

The earthquake, tsunami and malfunctioning nuclear plants in Japan have provided a world stage, demonstrating the resiliency and kindness of the Japanese people, even while in survival mode, caring for one another despite their dire circumstances. Those in the hardest hit areas are sharing whatever they still have, elder workers are volunteering to go back to the nuclear plants so that the younger ones won't have to, and in some stores people are buying less food supplies than they think they might need so that there will be enough for others to purchase. In shelters, even people who are receiving aid are reallocating what they've been given so that no one goes without. The people of Japan are an inspiring example of reaching out to and attending to each other at a time when everyone's needs are overwhelming.

The next stories take place at different times and locations, but are nonetheless poignant for the depiction of individuals motivated to give and to receive comfort in chaos.

Army of Volunteers

Marilyn is no stranger to adversity. While in the midst of some of the most challenging and life-threatening situations, she has discovered how resilient she could be and how willing others are to help. She has experienced firsthand the kindness of people, often total strangers, and says she'll never forget what that felt like.

In August 1997, Marilyn and her husband, Mike, nearly lost their home to a fire. Forced to flee with only the clothes on their backs and a handful of work clothes, Marilyn says, "As I stood there watching our house burn, knowing that almost every material thing that I owned could be gone, I thought, *We're all okay, and that's all that matters.*"

Someone generously offered them a place to stay, while others pitched in with clothes and other necessary items. A friend washed their clothes daily. Eventually, they were able to move back home, but the experience had created a shift in perspective and values, which helped when facing the next crisis.

On October 29, 2005, Hurricane Katrina wrought havoc and caused severe flooding that claimed over 1,800 lives in New Orleans, where Mike and Marilyn had lived for twenty-two years. Once again forced to evacuate their home and dependent on the kindness of others, they were welcomed in the homes of several family members while they waited out the storm. Three weeks later, as they were making their way back home, Hurricane Rita struck New Orleans.

"Being displaced is incredibly stressful, especially when there's no phone service, and we didn't know which of our friends made it out safely and which ones didn't," Marilyn says. "There's a hierarchy of de-stressing news: First it's a relief to know that everyone is alive. Then it's gratifying to find out that everyone got out safely. Finally, you can worry about your home and whether it survived the storm."

Wherever she went, Marilyn met people who wanted to help. At one chain clothing store, she was offered a discount on her purchases. A customer in the store, who happened to be the same size, overheard and immediately went to her car to get a box of lovely clothes, which she handed to Marilyn.

Even the smallest acts of kindness lifted her spirits. "Twice I needed a haircut and the hair stylists refused to charge me when they heard about my loss," Marilyn says. "People everywhere offered their homes, food, and whatever they had to share. When my daughter and her family were displaced after having lost everything, my cousin and my sister filled my daughter's vehicle with batteries, flashlights, towels, dishes, and necessities to set up a home. En route to their destination, they stayed at a hotel in Atlanta and were not charged a thing."

It was not always reported in the news, but Marilyn was amazed at the numerous churches and an *army of volunteers* from all over the country who helped people clean out their homes and rebuild. "People's generosity was astounding."

"Throughout the ordeal, I never felt afraid," Marilyn says. "I was deeply touched by the graphic examples of people's willingness to go out of their way to help. That kindness and support has given me a new awareness of how I want to be in the world. I now look at my life as having more possibilities to do things for others, and I'm grateful for each opportunity."

♡ *Have you ever been involved in a flood, fire, or natural disaster?*

♡ *If so, did that experience change your perception about the kindness of people?*

♡ *What would it feel like to be dependent on others for your basic needs of food, clothing or shelter?*

♡ *If you were in a place where you didn't know anyone and needed assistance, would you trust that someone would help you?*

Nice Planet to Live On

From their living room, Cheryl and Rich watched the live news broadcast of the human tragedy taking place in New Orleans in the immediate aftermath of Hurricane Katrina.

Rich, an auto mechanic, said, "I have four weeks' vacation time coming to me."

Cheryl, who works at a bank, looked at him and said, "I have three."

"Let's go!"

The following morning, they packed up their vehicle with sleeping bags, food, and supplies, and drove hundreds of miles to Louisiana, where they joined thousands of volunteers from all over the country and world.

Just the year before, Rich and Cheryl had been enjoying the jazz festival in New Orleans when Rich had become deathly ill with viral meningitis and was rushed to nearby Slidel Memorial Hospital. "We were blown away by the kindness and hospitality that we received before, during and after that memorable hospital stay. We were treated as though we had lived there all of our lives, like family," Cheryl says. "What we have learned about the people of Louisiana is that they are wired to help and never expect it to be paid back. How could we not go when our friends needed help?"

Cheryl and Rich didn't know what to expect when they

arrived. What they found were people helping people in any way that they could. It didn't matter what you did for a living; what mattered was that you were able to lend a helping hand. One family had immediately donated about seven acres of land towards creating a relief camp. A "Bob Marley look-alike," who had lost his home to the floods, volunteered to drive a Red Cross truck to deliver food to neighbors and those in need.

Several times, when volunteers arrived at someone's home to muck it out, the owner would direct them to a friend or neighbor's home instead: "Eunice's house down the street is much worse."

Cheryl says that many of the homes looked like the roof had been taken off and a gigantic mix master had been put in, shaking everything in all directions." They might find a refrigerator in the living room and mud and debris covering someone's precious lifetime possessions.

Rich and Cheryl were struck by one man's journey all the way from India to help out. Arun had been just a young boy in Bhopal when the Union Carbide explosion killed thousands of people there. His world had been destroyed then, but he'd remembered two things: "the U.S. Air Force symbols on the planes that brought in relief supplies and the funny English accents of the people who handed out candy bars and whatever they had that we needed."

It took Arun about five years to discover that it was the Louisiana Air National Guard that had arrived to take care of them after the disaster. Now, many years later, he says, "When I saw on the news what was happening to the people of Louisiana, I felt an absolute compulsion to pay it back."

The volunteers in New Orleans came from many directions and represented all walks of life. Rich loved the fact that each person offered their talents and prioritized the needs of others, "without having anyone barking out orders. We worked from sunrise to sunset, but weren't tired."

Overall, Rich found it to be an incredible lifetime experience that he wouldn't trade for anything. "I was really cynical about our country until I experienced Katrina," Rich confesses. "It totally changed my outlook. After weeks of witnessing the unrelenting human kindness, I thought, *Maybe I do live on a nice planet after all!*"

♡ *What would it be like to have just lost your home and a lifetime of treasured possessions?*

♡ *In what ways would you want others to respond to you?*

♡ *Would you share your possessions or home with those who have experienced such losses? How would you choose to offer your assistance?*

Global Neighborhood

To love one's country is natural,
but why must it end at that border.

— Pablo Cassals

When I was growing up, my parents told me, "Finish your vegetables, because poor people are starving." Their admonishment didn't mean much to me because I had never seen someone starving in China or India or anywhere. Today, because of cable television and the Internet, we regularly see the hungry faces of people in other countries in our living rooms, kitchens, and classrooms. It makes the plight of others more tangible.

Global has become local. As our awareness has expanded, we are experiencing a universal connection that can transform everyone into a neighbor with the click of a button.

Is anyone really so far away? Even if people look different than we do, are they really? Don't they ache like we do when they lose a loved one? Don't they suffer if they lose their homes or businesses? And don't they feel despair when they're hungry, sick, lonely, or weary? It's evident that our neighbors are everywhere, and we all need each other's help.

With each world crisis, we are reminded that in one moment our lives can change. In one moment we could lose all that we love and hold dear. The Japanese people, who share the same moon, sun, and planet as we do, experienced a series of moments when the earth and waters shifted and thousands of lives were lost, while thousands more were changed forever. Our fellow world citizens are hungry, weary, injured, and have lost their loved ones, homes, and even entire villages.

We don't have to belong to the same family, community, neighborhood, or country to extend a helping hand, to offer financial, physical, or emotional support. In fact, we are all part of one tribe: It's called the human race. Millions of us throughout the world share a heart connection as we join in prayers for the health, safety and well-being of the victims of Japan's natural and man-made disasters, and other tragedies around the globe.

When we witness the pain and suffering of others with open hearts and hold them in our thoughts and prayers, the flow of loving energy doesn't take into account where someone lives, what they look like, or what they do for a living. In fact, we might never meet in person. We are one loving heart touching another; the feelings of compassion are the same.

Regardless of religious or spiritual beliefs, we have come to realize that what we do for or to each other matters. As our concept of neighborhood expands to global proportions, we express our *currency of love* by simply seeing a need and doing our best to meet it. In doing so, we discover and experience the sense of *oneness* that almost all religions speak about—a connection to the divine source of life itself—and we are all equal participants.

The following stories are about people who live without

cultural or geographical boundaries. They have no hesitation about extending a helping hand to their neighbors, whoever and wherever they may be.

One Box Makes All the Difference

Raised by a single mom, Beverly Hill grew up with a supportive network of strong, independent women who encouraged her to do whatever she set her mind to. Inspired by these matriarchal role models, whose work involved helping others, Beverly chose to spend her free time in high school as a volunteer with the local Emergency Medical Services. While most teens were hanging out at the local soda shop, Beverly spent almost every weekend riding along in ambulances and participating in community-based events.

Many years later, Beverly's friends applauded, but were not surprised by, her decision to put her life and work on her Ph.D. aside to personally respond to the human suffering caused by Haiti's earthquake.

In her own words, Beverly shares her experience as a ShelterBox volunteer:

It's a surreal entry into Port au Prince from the air, as a vast landscape emerges, dotted with tent camps, fallen buildings and people lining main streets. Amid the contoured shapes of tarps, sheets, and other makeshift dwellings, there are very few vehicles in motion.

It's my fourth visit to Haiti as a SRT (ShelterBox Response Team) volunteer, to assist in the ongoing mission of providing shelter, warmth, and dignity to the survivors of the catastrophic earthquake. We've been well-received by the Haitian communities, who understand that the "big green box" that we're there to deliver is full of more than just a tent, water purification system, cook stove, sleeping pads, tool kit, and other basic essentials—it's an offering of hope.

Moving through immigration and customs, my face stands out

among the sea of Haitian locals. Two young Haitian men greet me as I walk to the arrival area. They smile as big as they can as they notice my T-shirt and shout, "ShelterBox!"

In many areas of Port au Prince, makeshift dwellings are erected upon every spare bit of land in and around this oversized, overburdened, and collapsed city. People still shower in tarp-covered stalls along main roads, and bathe in small tubs that are a fraction of their body size. They sleep in small dwellings among others, some of whom they barely know. The rubble that once was their home still sits piled up in the same place that it fell on January 12, 2010. The power and water supply is inconsistent, and jobs are even scarcer than they were prior to the earthquake. The simplest of things bring the greatest joy to these individuals, who live in the most poverty-stricken country in the southern hemisphere.

Joey, a young man whom I meet one day, speaks better English than many of the other community members, and strikes up a conversation with me. I notice his uniform and ask if his school has resumed since the earthquake hit four months earlier. "Yes," he says, with the most amazing smile, "but I have come here because I know you have brought for my family a tent." Fifteen years old, Joey has assumed responsibility for his parents and siblings. At the risk of missing the first day of school, he is here because of his hope that his family, among the thousands of other families displaced by disaster, will be one of the fortunate ones to receive a box. I have learned that one box can make all the difference in getting on with life.

What is alarming to me since my last visit more than six months ago is that conditions have improved very little in some places, while they have worsened in others. But on this trip, I'm able to hear some of the personal stories of how ShelterBox has made a difference in the lives of many Haitians.

Goudou, a tailor in his thirties, lives in a medium-size camp and uses his ShelterBox tent not only as a home, but also as a place to set up his sewing machine. Each day, under the hot Haitian sun, he's able to make clothing and textiles for his neighbors and members of his community.

In the over-crowded downtown area of Port au Prince, the head nurse at a tuberculosis clinic states that without the two tents that we'd delivered, the nurses wouldn't have space to work or be able to attend to the patients' needs.

Then there are the women of Kofaviv, who have survived domestic and sexual abuse. Without a ShelterBox tent, they would have no other place to go. The tents provide not only a home, but also protection.

In meeting many of the volunteers, I sometimes wonder what moves people to reach out to a population of individuals seemingly so different from their own culture. For me, it's quite simple: It's the recognition that at our core, we are all the same. We all desire and deserve to be loved and cared for, we all have the same basic needs for survival, and we all have dreams for a better future.

What I've learned from these Haitian members of my global family is that love is what prevails. We've become their friends, and in some cases an extended family, and they've become ours.

ShelterBox has just completed the longest deployment in their history: providing 27,000 boxes to shelter more than 250,000 Haitians. Beverly has now become a spokesperson for Shelter Box.

♡ *Although you may not be able to offer physical help during a disaster, in what other ways can you offer hope and support?*

♡ *What are your strengths and limitations in how you can contribute to others?*

♡ *Are you able to find that place within yourself that understands that there is no difference between you and your neighbor, whoever and wherever they may be?*

Firefighters with Compassion

When a group of fourteen big-hearted firefighters in Sarasota County, Florida, learned that their counterparts in Nicaragua lacked not only training, but also essential firefighting equipment, they decided to personally jump on board to help. Not knowing what to expect, they each committed to giving a week of their time, their energy, and experience, plus $1,000 of their own money to cover their expenses, while in Nicaragua. They also asked for donations and the community generously responded.

Assistant Chief Mary Boutieller says, "I sent out a personal e-mail to friends letting them know what we needed, and was astounded by the generosity of people who gave money or left items on my doorstep daily, oftentimes without letting on who they were."

Each firefighter, who made the trip, carried two fifty-pound suitcases filled with $5,000 to $6,000 worth of hoses, nozzles, and other equipment, as well as clothes and shoes donated by numerous individuals and businesses in Florida and elsewhere. Battalion Chief T.J. Broom, who initiated the trip with the support of Forward Edge International, says the group received a hero's welcome from more than sixty volunteer firefighters when they arrived in Managua, Nicaragua.

They spent the first three days training the Nicaraguan firefighters in such basics as CPR and extrication procedures. The following heart-wrenching days were spent in La Chureca, a Managua dump that is home to some 3,000 people, many of whom live in cardboard shacks. T.J. says. "We met one extended family of sixteen people living in a 600-square foot home."

"It was difficult to watch as children and adults picked through the garbage daily for food," Mary adds. "We were told that many of these girls, as young as nine or ten years old, would become prostitutes, as their families bartered their daughters for favors from the garbage truck drivers, usually to get first choice of the scraps."

The team helped one family who had been ostracized because the mother and father had AIDS, and no one would venture near them or their four young children. The volunteers helped to clean their cardboard abode and to wash the children's ailing father.

People lined up by the hundreds, thankful to receive the clothes and shoes the team had brought for them. T.J. was deeply touched by the children who survive on so little, "I love these kids. They are so grateful for one outfit, a notebook and a toy, that you would think that you had just bought them a car!" Considering that the average yearly income in Managua is only $800, abundance takes on a whole new meaning.

The firefighters spent their remaining time shoveling rock and pouring concrete to help complete "Villa Esperanza" (Village of Hope), where seventy-two girls would eventually live. Mary Boutieller says, "We did anything they asked us to do, as hard as we could and as best we could."

The firefighters were gratified to know that some of the young girls would have a better life because of their efforts. When the father with AIDS died shortly after it was completed, his two young daughters were placed at Villa Esperanza, where they would have a clean bed, regular meals, the use of a playground, and the opportunity to receive an education. It's an effort that will continue to make a difference. In fact, T.J. Broom's teenage daughter, Jessie, plans to join a church youth group to help build more houses for the girls.

"What we are doing with the villa is just awesome," says T.J. "One of the things about Nicaragua is that it's not just about the work, it's about the relationships. It's tough to explain, but when I'm leaving there, I'm already thinking about when I'm coming back."

At the end of the long, productive week, volunteer Lieutenant John Hanlon summed up their experience: "I've been a paid firefighter for thirty-one years, and I've never felt prouder to be one than when I was in the Managua station. It reminded me why we're firefighters—because we get more out of it than we give."

♡ *What moves you to offer help either monetarily or in person when you witness people's need in other countries?*

♡ *While some people are better prepared to give physical help than others, what are the ways that you would want to offer your support and encouragement?*

♡ *Is there a charity that you like to donate to that matches your philosophy of giving?*

♡ *Can you relate to the pain of someone who looks or acts differently than you?*

Gift of Light

Did you know that in the developing world, 2.4 billion people, a third of the population of the planet, do not have access to clean, affordable light? There are people living in villages around the world who still rely primarily on kerosene lanterns, candles, and battery-powered flashlights for light. These sources of light are expensive, dangerous, and harmful to the environment; they also have a negative impact on people's health, education, and security.

That information was all it took to arouse the compassion of Neil Cohen, an entrepreneur who had been seeking ways to give back. "For many years, I had been inspired by the visionary ideas and humanitarian expression that brought benefit to others in the world," he says. "I realized that I didn't want to live my life solely for my self-oriented desires and goals. I wanted to do something more meaningful and of value to others."

When one is on an altruistic path, one project often leads serendipitously to another. Neil had founded Source Point Global Outreach, a non-profit with a mission to serve the welfare of our global family. Its initial and ongoing commitment is to bring self-help resources and teachings of compassion and nonviolence to men and women in U.S. prisons. However, it was while he was selling solar-powered flashlights online to raise money for this project that Neil learned of the many people throughout the world who lacked safe and affordable lighting. He recognized the opportunity to use his resources to improve the lives of many impoverished people in places such as Tibet, India, and Africa.

So, Neil founded the *Solar Light Project*, which uses 100 percent of the monies it collects to purchase and send solar-powered lights to outreach organizations, who give them directly to families in remote villages without electricity. A flashlight that costs only five dollars is a priceless tool that can satisfy the varied needs of generations of villagers: It allows people to read and study at night, benefits the elderly whose vision is impaired, and aids farmers who have to care for their animals in the dark.

Meet some of the people who are grateful for this simple gift of light:

Niang is a young mother who knows that the only hope for a better life for her children is through education. Her children attend school after their farm chores are done. They often have to walk home at night, causing Niang to worry until they arrive safely. Once at home, lack of light keeps them from studying or doing their homework. The solar flashlights offer a wonderful solution to this family's needs.

In one Tibetan village, seventeen children ranging in age from seven to thirteen walk five kilometers to go to school. Because the walk takes some forty minutes, they need to leave at 6 a.m., when it is so dark that they can barely see the road. The flashlights they received are invaluable to ensure their safety, and to enable the very youngest children, who are intimidated by the dark, to attend school.

At seventy-two, Mrs. Shen is elderly and frail. She is one of many elders who are fearful of falling down the cement stairs outside of their homes when they have to navigate the darkness or use the toilet at night. A light provides immeasurable comfort, convenience, and safety.

Perched on the highest mountain slopes in China's Sichuan province, twenty-seven families received flashlights. These villagers use the flashlights to make traveling at night safer. One farmer expressed his gratitude in a letter: "Generally our living condition is very poor and hard to live since it is rural and no good income resource. So the flashlights are very useful for us because we have no electricity and we can just charge it by sunshine without paying anything."

Even the volunteers with other service organizations have benefited from the use of the flashlights. Stationed in Africa, one volunteer reported he most certainly would have stepped on a deadly, poisonous snake were it not for the glow his flashlight cast on the rapidly slithering form.

To date, Neil Cohen has shipped about 1,700 gifts of light, at no charge, to grateful villagers, though it's merely a drop in a sea of needs. He is touched by the individual expressions of appreciation that he receives on a regular basis. "The photographs and letters speak all the words necessary," says Neil. "Seeing people's surprised and happy faces as they receive the solar flashlights is deeply gratifying. Just the simple act of offering something that brings happiness and benefit to others is all the reward I could ever want."

♡ *Have you ever experienced a blackout, where you had to do everything by candlelight and flashlight? What would it have been like if you had no electricity for your computer, television, or refrigerator for weeks or months at a time?*

♡ *How would you feel if you couldn't afford to have light for your children to walk safely home from school or to be able to study in the evenings?*

♡ *Can you imagine what it would be like to receive a gift of a solar flashlight that would offer you and your family safe and inexpensive lighting?*

A Good Guest of the Planet

*Only when the last tree has died, the last river has been poisoned
and the last fish has been caught,
will we realize that we can't eat money.*

— Native American Cree proverb

Why is it that we tend to value people, places and things more when we are at risk of losing them? It seems that when there's plenty, we're less likely to appreciate and take care of what we have. And for many, it's only when we see the rivers drying up, the dead fish encased in oil on the shores, the dark brown cloud on the horizon, and the birds falling from the sky that we take notice.

While it's hard not to be aware of the negative impact that we've had on the Earth—air and water pollution, deforestation, etc.—imminent loss makes it more likely that we will take action to preserve what we have and to prevent further depletion of our natural resources.

Each thing that we do matters, especially when multiplied by the millions of people sharing this planet. Our decisions to recycle, to conserve water and natural resources, to drive less, to hold corporations who pollute accountable, and to support organizations and people who are leading the way in environmental consciousness and actions are all acts of kindness, not only to the planet and its current inhabitants, but to future generations as well.

A Good Guest

Recently, my friend, Jessie, and I were invited to stay at the beautiful home of a couple, whom we had literally met the night before, although we had close mutual friends.

I always feel a responsibility to be a *good guest*, which for me means bringing gifts of food or flowers, helping with cooking and chores, and being respectful, unobtrusive, and appreciative. And I try to leave someone's home in the same way, or better, for future guests to enjoy.

At the end of our stay, I expressed to Jessie my hope that I'd achieved "good guest status." She said, "You have. In fact, you're a good guest of the planet!"

The comment made me think about my temporary stay on Earth. Was I fully valuing the gift of living here, taking care of the earth and its resources as best I could? Was I taking no more than I needed, or more than I could give back? Was I leaving it in at least as good a state as it was when I arrived? Was I being respectful to its other inhabitants and sharing resources equitably?

While overall, I think I'm doing an okay job, it's people like Charles Tanner, in the following story, who garner my utmost respect for their extraordinary efforts to care for the environment as an honored guest on our planet.

Restoring my Carbon Footprint

Tall and muscular, Charles Tanner looks like he could easily survive off the land. Raised by parents who had lived through the 1930's depression, he learned at an early age the value of frugality and appreciation of limited resources. He spent time with his grandfather, a "tenant farmer," who scratched out an existence on the land, teaching young Charles how to grow things and handle a planting spade. To this day, Charles still finds deep satisfaction in transforming a piece of fallow land into a place of growth and renewal.

In his own words, Charles shares his amazing story:

Somewhere I read that the average person uses the equivalent of 900 trees in a lifetime. It made me think about all the disposable paper products and wood items that I was using. Once I realized the huge impact on our environment that's made by one person, I committed to making a concerted effort to put back at least 900 trees—my way of leaving a "zero tree footprint" as I journey on this beautiful planet.

Having had the woodsy bug in my blood for as long as I can remember, I often found myself seeking out rural landscapes in which to tramp and camp. You might say I became a self-taught "Grizzly Adams." As time passed, my wilderness skills grew.

While the tree project started out small, with ample plantings around my home, before long, I was also planting trees in the yards of friends and relatives. I found a tree farm program and purchased seedlings in bulk quantities at very reasonable rates.

As luck would have it, I worked for an environmental firm, which allowed me to utilize my skills demonstrating and teaching others how to plant acreage from cleared forest regions, as well as how to reforest former hazardous waste sites in the Midwest.

Soon, I found that I was eagerly using up all of my weekends and vacation time purchasing and developing tracts of former farmland to create budding (no pun intended) tree farms. I even took up residence on some of these properties by erecting a makeshift, humble home for myself.

It felt like my own Walden Pond experience. I cooked and ate over open fires and bathed in ponds and creeks, never missing the comforts of home. I used a combination of primitive and modern tools to eke out an existence from these small plots of land.

It was a labor of love. I would mow, mow, and mow some more, clearing the land and planting trees as I went, row by row. It was unbelievably strenuous, and I'm certain that I worked harder on those long weekends than at any job I'd ever had.

And so it was that I planted those 900 trees and didn't know how to stop. Soon my seedlings numbered in the thousands. The years passed and those numbers continued to grow. What began as a forty-four acre project soon grew into 280 acres—nature's canvas, if you will, with my arms and tools as the paint and brushes.

One fall I got to visit some of the trees that I had planted twenty years before. I walked the pathway lined with 8 inch tree trunks soaring majestically upward and felt a vibration that radiated to my core. I was humbled to know I had helped God out just a little, making good on some of the things I had taken in life.

I'm proud to have been a contributor to our planet and not just a consumer. It would be an accurate statement to say that in serving mankind and nature, I have touched hundreds of thousands of trees. It's a legacy that I believe will offer benefits long after I'm fertilizer, perhaps for some of those very trees.

♡ *In what ways do you consider yourself a good guest of the planet?*

♡ *How can you protect and replenish the Earth's resources?*

♡ *What's one thing that you can do that would have a positive impact now?*

♡ *What is the legacy you would like to leave for future inhabitants of the planet?*

Nine

Feeding A Passion

Don't ask what the world needs.
Ask what makes you come alive and go do it.
Because what the world needs is people who have come alive.

— Howard Thurman

What is it that enlivens you, that you find joy in expressing, and that you would do for free because it's what nourishes you and gives meaning and fulfillment to your life? Most of us feel fortunate when we have such a passion —that quality of aliveness and intensity.

For some people it might be their job, for some a creative endeavor, and for others, it is in giving. People who are passionate about giving respond to the needs of others as to a calling. They are as committed and generous in their expressions of love and kindness as someone else might be about offering their gifts as an artist, writer, or teacher.

One time, I took a drawing class taught by an artist who told us: "I HAVE TO draw! I draw on anything that is available to me —paper bags, the back of a baseball ticket, a receipt ... wherever I am." And that's how it is with passionate givers—they can't walk by someone needing help and not respond. For these individuals, giving is a *currency of love* that is as natural as breathing.

While there are unlimited choices in how people can contribute to others, whether it be a one-time occurrence or ongoing acts of giving, the individuals in this chapter are finding and expressing their passion in ways that can contribute to others and feed their soul. Whether big or small, each story is inspiring in how they, ordinary people, are touching and changing lives.

A Lifetime of Generosity

I shall pass this way but once;
any good, therefore, that I can do
or any kindness that I can show to any fellow being,
let me do it now.
Let me not deter or neglect it,
as I shall not pass this way again.

– William Penn

The diversity of the next two stories, from a woman who lives like a nun to a renaissance man whose life is a work of art, exemplifies that we each have our own unique path and way to measure our wealth and express our *currency of love.*

Not only do these individuals share an irresistible urge to give, but they do it consistently throughout their lives. They seem to find endless opportunities for assisting others no matter where they are. Their acts of generosity are simply who they are and what they do. Giving brings them as much joy and fulfillment as it enriches the lives of the people they help.

Those who have been natural givers their entire lives embody the adage that the joy of giving is a gift that needs no acknowledgment or reward. Their lives are rich and full beyond measure.

Out of Thankfulness

"We make a living by what we get;
we make a life by what we give."
– Winston Churchill

Pauline Benoit (*Aunt Pepine* to me and her numerous nieces and nephews) has had a desire to serve in her French Catholic church since she was seven years old. She lived across the street from the convent then and assisted the nuns by cleaning, fixing books, washing blackboards, and doing anything else that was needed. She says, "A nun would put a flag in the window of the convent as a signal to me that she needed help running errands, and off I would go!

"I've always found it natural helping and doing things for others," Pauline says. In addition to working a full-time job until retirement, she has continued her volunteer work in the church for seventy-seven years. "My greatest joy is doing God's work. It's what keeps me happy and keeps me going." At eight-four years of age, she still has a youthful look and demeanor. In fact, her natural, rich brown hair has never been colored. (Of course, her nieces tell her that's because she never married!)

Pauline lives directly across the street from her church in Southbridge, Massachusetts.

Walking into her house is like entering a shrine. Everyday she descends and climbs three flights of stairs to clean pews, set up for mass, wash the altar cloths, and bring communion to people who are ill. She prays for people in need, believing that prayers are powerful and can move mountains. "There are so many people on my prayer list," she says, adding, "sometimes I forget to pray for myself."

When church officials offered to put her on the payroll for her numerous hours of service, Pauline put her foot down. "If you put me on the payroll, I'm not coming back! I thank God every day for what I've been able to do. I do things out of thankfulness."

Aunt Pepine is kind and loving no matter what happens in her life, and for me it validates a *currency of love* and goodness that is real and constant.

♡ *What are you passionate about and how do you express and share it?*

♡ *Do you know someone who has lived a life serving others?*

♡ *Does their dedication to others inspire you with hope for a better world?*

♡ *Are there ways that you like to offer your service to others?*

Convicted of Kindness

> *If you were arrested for kindness,*
> *would there be enough evidence to convict you?*
> – Author unknown

Despite his thirteen years as a Florida Supreme Court-certified mediator, volunteering his skills toward conflict resolution, there is no question that David Gittens (a.k.a. Dwij) would not only be arrested, but locked up for being a serial perpetrator of loving acts of kindness. He has a passion for giving that permeates everything that he does, so that even if he were paroled, he would go right back to his habitual ways of treating everyone with love, generosity, and respect.

Here is evidence to indicate that David would have no choice but to enter a guilty plea:

Starting out as a Boy Scout in Brooklyn, David has been performing acts of kindness and service right up to his seventy-second year on this terrestrial stage.

Simple things, like helping a friend to locate tires for her car or taking fresh-picked tangerines from his tree to residents at a senior center on his weekly visits, as well as major projects such as the creation of *The Giving Tree* (a community holiday program providing educational gifts and soft toys to youngsters from impoverished families) make up the framework for a lifetime of community involvement.

David designed and built safe and innovative playgrounds for schools in northern California, and following this, he went to live with the Mayans in Guatemala, where he planned and designed a solar heated community shower system funded with a UNICEF grant.

David is a true "Renaissance man"—a modern day Da Vinci. His scientific life and creative work have always been geared towards helping others rather than focused on making money. Although he doesn't have material wealth, he says, "I think I'm one of the richest people in terms of the gifts I've been given and have been able to share … and I'm just getting started."

Even his business ventures, such as the design of the Ikenga automobiles and autogiro aircraft have had an underlying intention of benefiting community, whether through the creation of jobs for locals, or in the case of the autogiro, through fulfilling utility needs of many in Third World cultures.

David is committed to making a difference in his community. He produced an online publication to promote the writings of local and worldwide contributors on topics ranging from health and wellness to spirituality, mediation, and children's visions of world peace.

Thirteen years ago, he and a few friends started a drumming circle on Siesta Key Beach, which continues to draw some 75 to 100 people every Sunday night. For six years he facilitated a monthly networking group at a local restaurant. Currently, he is hosting a men's meditation circle, described by one six-year-long member as: "a safe environment to experience camaraderie and a feeling of oneness, as we talk about our ups and downs, spirituality, and gratitude." And David loves to share another of his passions—the music of his heart, which he plays on a self-designed 23-string guitar at community concerts.

Although there is a great deal more evidence, no further testimonies are needed. It is quite clear that David would not only be arrested, but would be convicted of kindness.

♡ *If you were arrested for kindness, would there be enough evidence to convict you?*

♡ *How would your friends testify and describe their interactions with you?*

♡ *What are your unique expressions of kindness that would reveal your identity?*

Above and Beyond the Call of Duty

Your work is to discover your work and then with all your heart to give yourself to it.

— Buddha

Many people spend their waking hours at a job that they may or may not find satisfying. To many, "a job is just a job," a way to support themselves, their families, and their lifestyles. The hours away from their work are what offer them the time and freedom to explore and to do what they find meaningful.

For others, it is their career that allows them to feel fulfilled, doing life-affirming work that feeds their passion and gives them an opportunity to contribute. For these people, their work is not simply about the money, but is a way to express their creativity and talents to help others and to create a better world.

Here is the story of one man who finds such tremendous fulfillment in his job supporting veterans that he would "do it for free." And following that are stories of individual postal carriers who deliver much more than the mail.

Feeding His Soul

We make a living by what we get;
we make life by what we give.
– Winston Churchill

Pat Hall was a bit of a brawler before he joined the Marines at nineteen. That decision changed his life. He says, "In time, my experiences as a military police officer jolted my thinking and caused me to do some soul searching: Who was I and what did I stand for? In the end, I became an advocate for nonviolence."

Having completed his duty as a Marine corporal, Pat is passionate about his career as a supervisory veteran service representative, which allows him to continue serving his country. He assists hundreds of soldiers returning from Iraq and Afghanistan, as well as thousands of veterans from Vietnam, Korea, and even World War II, in obtaining disability and health-care benefits. "If the only thing I can do is to help deserving people to get hearing aids and monthly checks, then I'm honored to do it," he says. But he does so much more.

Pat puts in extra time and effort to ensure that these veterans, who have sacrificed so much for their country, get compensated quickly and efficiently. "If I work hard, there's a family that won't go hungry. It's the veteran's family, the kid in the back seat of the car, that motivates me to get these claims processed." In fact, he is proud of the fact that he consistently processes claims in far less time than the national average.

What Pat finds especially gratifying is to support those who have lost their limbs, health, confidence, and peace of mind. "The military and the VA make the seriously wounded the highest priority, but while many veterans are able to adapt to their circumstances over time and lead happy and healthy lives, there are many others who spend the rest of their lives suffering in their homes. Being homebound is something that many veterans suggest *feels like prison*."

As part of his job, Pat loves participating in the Winter Sports Clinic, held yearly in Colorado. It has successfully brought together almost 400 disabled veterans, getting them out of their houses, as well as their comfort zones. Skiing and other activities offer those who have been secluded a chance to connect with their buddies and to reclaim some of their athletic abilities that had been a natural part of being a soldier. "It's great to see veterans, who might normally be overlooked or avoided by society, fraternize with others in similar situations and just have fun," says Pat. "They go down those ski slopes with nothing but smiles."

Pat understands the hardships of being a soldier. He remembers watching his dad deploy a couple of times when he was a kid. He also knows what it's like to be the dad saying goodbye to a child; his son was born while he was in the Marines, and he only got to see his little boy three times before he turned two.

Leaving the Marines had been a rough adjustment for Pat, but in time he adapted. He now thrives on helping veterans make the transition from military to civilian life, and knows the transformation doesn't happen overnight. "It's tough coming home and adjusting to being a regular person again," Pat says. In the service, "there's a sense of camaraderie and trust in being a part of a unit that comes from knowing that someone is always watching your back and that no one will be left behind. Their buddies are often with them 24/7 and are closer to them than anyone else." That level of commitment and connection is hard to replicate in civilian life, and so veterans often feel isolated and alone.

Pat's family is well aware of the importance of maintaining that sense of connection. Pat, his parents, his wife, Kate, and their two sons, recently volunteered their Fourth of July weekend to support those in the Denver wheelchair races. Even Pat's three-year-old son Zach pitched in by playing catch with some of the veterans, bringing infectious smiles to many faces.

Pat believes that the most important thing that we, as a society, can do is to acknowledge these veterans for the sacrifices that they have made for our country. It's no less than he asks of himself.

"I love my work," Pat says. "It's like no other job in the world, and I would do it for free. It's what feeds my soul."

♡ *Do you know any veterans? When you see or meet a veteran, do you acknowledge them and let them know that they are appreciated?*

♡ *What is it that feeds your soul? Are you able to make a living doing what you love?*

♡ *What do you believe is more important—doing what you love now, even if it means taking less pay, or making enough money so that you can do what you love when you retire?*

"Through Rain, Sleet and . . . "

These days, more people are using alternatives to the U.S. Postal Service to pay bills and to keep in touch. Financial concerns mean the possibility of fewer days of mail-delivery service in the future.

But unlike many businesses that have become irrelevant in today's current environment where personal daily contact is rare, thousands of people still find the highlight of their day to be the greeting of their mail carrier.

It is to these dedicated individuals, who go beyond their job of delivering envelopes and packages, that I feel a debt of gratitude for making a difference in the lives of many people, especially the elderly.

Through rain, sleet, and lots of sunlight, Miguel, a friendly and courteous Florida mail carrier, brings even more sunshine to everyone on his route, as he delivers a smile, a good word, and a personal connection, along with the mail.

"When I see the mail stack up for the elderly people, I am concerned," Miguel says. "There's a woman in this condo complex that is 100 years old. She has people taking care of her, but when I noticed that her mail had not been picked up for several days, I bundled it and brought it directly to her. She was happy that I would personally bring her mail and spend time to talk with her, making sure she was okay."

Another mail carrier, Dan, has been delivering correspondence to some of the same people for more than twenty years. He is quick to share how appreciative they are for every little thing that he does for them. Dan thinks of many of his customers as family, and considers it a privilege to deliver their mail.

"There are three people on my route who are Holocaust survivors—they still have the branded numbers on their arms," says Dan. "They treat me with such respect, calling me 'sir,' when I am the one who feels honored to be able to serve them."

One elderly woman, whom Dan had gotten to like, didn't pick up her mail for a few days and he was concerned. He decided to unofficially investigate and went to the back of her house and peered in her windows. "I could see her lying unconscious on her kitchen floor, and I knew that I had to do something fast." Dan called a rescue team, who subsequently broke into her home and saved her life. The woman's relatives were so grateful that Dan is now a regular part of their family gatherings.

Years earlier, in a different part of the country, another postal carrier likely saved a life:

Iris, a large woman, was distressed when she realized that she was stuck in the bathtub, unable to get out. Living alone had its challenges, not the least of which was getting help when it was needed. For three days, with no rescue options in sight, Iris sat in the tub and kept herself occupied by wadding up toilet paper into spitballs and tossing them into the wastebasket.

Fortunately for Iris, her postal carrier noticed that her mail had not been retrieved for those three days; he decided to deliver it personally and make sure that she was alright. Iris was able to shout out to him in response to his knocking and was soon rescued.

These examples of caring are just a few reasons that I am grateful for the U.S. Postal Service carriers. May they continue to bring acknowledgment and personal contact to our computer-saturated lives.

♡ *Great Britain has a wonderful custom called "Boxer Day" (the day after Christmas), when you acknowledge everyone who provides service to you during the year, with money or a gift of appreciation.*

♡ *During the holidays, what special way do you have of remembering your postal carrier, newspaper delivery person or others who have taken care of you throughout the year?*

♡ *How can you extend it a step further by acknowledging those who provide you service at other times of the year —with a" thank you," a note of appreciation, homemade cookies ... or simply asking how their day is going?*

Life Beyond Retirement

It is one of the most beautiful compensations of this life that no person can sincerely try to help another, without helping himself.

– Ralph Waldo Emerson

Many people are finding new meaning in life as they conclude their careers, including *Baby Boomers* who are just beginning to discover what retirement looks like. With free time and energy, these retirees find fulfillment as they pursue the dreams that had been put on the back burner, explore unknown places, and find ways to make a difference in their communities and world.

And as they share their experience and knowledge, presence and passion, they are reinventing themselves, finding value in who they are, in contrast to the validation that they once received for the jobs that they performed or the people and careers they managed.

Living among a huge population of retirees inspires me. I meet people in their sixties through upper nineties whose lives are enriched by any number of volunteer activities: teaching, mentoring, opening schools in other countries, working in homeless shelters … giving of themselves in ways that weren't possible when they were raising a family or growing a business. These retirees are contributing thousands of hours of valuable service to nonprofits, their communities, neighborhoods, country, and world.

Shelly celebrated her 60th birthday in Jordan as a Peace Corp volunteer working with handicapped children. "What turns me on is working with kids," she says. And it doesn't matter who or where they are. Now, two years later, Shelly is living in a retirement community in Sonora, Mexico, where she finds joy teaching English two to three days a week to a group of children in a nearby, impoverished fishing village. The informal sessions, initially taking place under a palapa, are voluntary, but you can't keep the kids away when Shelly shows up.

She has inspired trust in those who have observed her dedication to the children, and was recently invited to share the one room school house. There Shelly saw the dire need for school supplies, and learned that if the community raised 10,000 pesos (about $850) they qualified to receive matching funds from the government to support their school. She contacted her friend, Diana, in Colorado, who put out the word to other friends, and within days they had raised most of the money needed. Shelly was delighted with the purchases made with these funds: white boards, markers, crayons and writing materials, as well as enough books to create a little library for the children, ages six to twelve. What is even more important is her message to these children that they matter.

The following story represents one example of a retiree making a difference. It's about a high-spirited octogenarian who finds fulfillment in volunteer traveling abroad.

At Home in the World

Dorothy Conlon was born in Japan to missionary parents, setting the stage for an adventuresome life of travel. As she tells her stories, it's obvious that Dorothy has lived a fulfilling and rich life, touching many people along her journey.

That journey hasn't always been easy. The death of her two sons in previous years made the 1989 loss of her husband, Ned, especially difficult. While working through her grief, she spent the next year in Thailand, where she volunteered through WorldTeach to work in a Thai government school in Bangkok. She hasn't stopped traveling since, teaching and doing volunteer work at home and abroad.

Dorothy has worked on 23 projects in 15 different countries, not only through volunteer organizations, but also through things that she has "cooked up." While most of the projects involve teaching English, she also helped to build a brick home for a teacher in Tanzania.

Dorothy says, "I'm not very good with languages, but I've never had trouble communicating." There's a universal language of the heart.

"My motivation for volunteering overseas is actually selfish, because it's so much fun," she says. "It gives me a totally different perspective of the people and the country, and when I can be of help, I'm grateful." She delights in portraying a different side of Americans than most natives see on television. Laughing, Dorothy says, "I love to see the shocked look on the faces of the locals when they experience someone my age, with sleeves rolled up and hands in the dirt, working right alongside of them."

Commenting on her trip to Ecuador to teach English at an elementary school, she says, "The beautiful part was staying for two weeks with a Quichua farm family. Living with a native host family allows you to gain great insights into the people and their way of life."

Each day she would walk for twenty minutes and then take a fifteen-minute bus ride to get to the school. However, at an altitude of almost 9,000 feet, the return walk home, on steep, muddy roads, turned into a forty-five-minute trek. "At eighty-two, I must admit that I had to stop a lot along the way to catch my breath."

Dorothy recently returned from a trip to the Dominican Republic, where she spent the first two weeks teaching English as a second language to fifth through eighth graders. She didn't know anyone before she left, but she feels that she made some great connections, and says, "I think my most positive effect was with the young volunteers, college or even high school age, who were fascinated that someone of my age would still be roaming around to different parts of the world, living simply, while volunteering."

Locally, Dorothy has been bringing the essence of her travels, in the form of slide shows, to retirement and nursing homes since 1993. In fact, she is about to present her 800th slide show. And she shares her adventures with a broader audience in her book, *At Home in the World: Memoirs of a Traveling Woman.* Dorothy says, "It's a joy to me to be able to share the wealth of my travel experiences with others." Not sure how much longer she will be able to travel, she intends to squeeze in as many travel adventures as she can.

♡ *At this stage in your life, what gives your life meaning and fulfillment?*

♡ *What would you like to contribute or share with others when you are retired or have more free time?*

♡ *What is the gift that you would like to leave for future generations?*

♡ *How can you begin the process of creating a valuable legacy now, one conversation and one action at a time?*

Ten

Energy of Giving and Receiving

"You give but little when you give of your possessions.
It is when you give of yourself that you truly give."

– Kahlil Gibran

Whatever we put out into the world—thoughts, actions, words or energy—comes back to us multiplied. We want to make sure that what we give out or take in is positive, and that it has a circular, rather than a one-way flow of energy. For example, when we refuse to accept gifts from others it blocks the circular flow of energy—there is only an outflow.

Ernest Holmes, the founder of *Science of Mind* stated, "When the law of circulation is retarded, stagnation results." That stuck energy can come from negative thoughts, self-motivated intentions, or the refusal or inability to give and receive with equanimity.

The *law of attraction* states that what you focus on is what you draw into your life. Sometimes the best way to get more of what you want in your life is to give away whatever you want to receive, whether it is kindness, love, compassion, or your currency of choice. When you give freely and joyfully from your heart, sharing your time, knowledge, resources and energy, according to the law of attraction, it will come back to you in abundance.

What you get back, though, may come to you indirectly, in unexpected ways, or from people that you don't know. It may show up in the form of things you need, people that cross your path at the right time, or money that turns up just when you need it.

While "giving" is considered a virtue, we often forget that it's equally important to be able to receive from others, so that they are allowed to participate in the same circular flow of giving and receiving.

The other day, my friend Jessie and I were walking into town when I noticed a man sitting on a stool on the sidewalk, with some kind of a folding tray in front of him, against which leaned a sign: VETERAN. Just before reaching him, I searched my purse for the loose dollar bill that I had seen earlier, having left my wallet in the car. I couldn't find it, but I wanted to give him something. I dug deep and found some loose coins in the bottom of my bag. I walked up to him, half apologizing that I didn't have more to offer.

Wearing a torn tee shirt, his weathered, but ruggedly handsome face, broke into a smile as he accepted the change. When I turned to leave, he said, "Wait, I want to give this to you," and he handed me a scroll. "It's my artwork." I was touched by his gracious giving and desire to share something special with me.

As Jessie and I walked away I said, "I wish I could at least find that dollar bill." I reached once more into the purse and there it was. I was so happy to turn around and offer it to him, and we smiled at each other, grateful for the heart exchange.

Jessie and I continued our walk to town, and she commented, "Wow, what an awesome experience!" In just a few moments, giver and receiver (and I'm not even sure which was which), as well as the witness were changed. When we got to the car and I opened the scroll, there was a beautiful drawing of a dove, a cross, and a crown of thorns, along with the artist's story of redemption.

And it doesn't stop there. Jessie admired the scroll, which will soon find its way into the gift bag with her other birthday presents.

Flow of Generosity

Without receivers, there can be no givers.

– Linda Maree

Giving in any form makes you feel rich, but especially when giving from the heart. The more you give, the better you feel, and so you are likely to give even more.

Studies have shown it's usually the giver who reaps the highest psychological benefit from the exchange. But is this innate or conditioned? Assuming this is a conditioned response, learned through repeated reminders of the "joy of giving," it seems reasonable that we could also learn the "joy of receiving." And if it is an innate characteristic, why wouldn't we allow others the chance to experience joy by letting them give to us?

It may be difficult to receive with graciousness and ease when one has been raised to believe that "it's better to give than to receive," or from a puritanical perspective, "you need to work for what you get."

Somewhere along the way, we may have gotten the message that the more powerful and better position to be in is that of the giver, whereas, the recipient is seen as needier or weaker. As the giver, we choose how, when, and what to give. Oftentimes, the recipient feels an unspoken debt that needs to be acknowledged or paid back, even when they didn't get what they wanted, needed, or even asked for.

In our quid pro quo society, one can't assume that a gift is given with no strings attached. A newly married young woman was asked by her in-laws to keep a list of the people who gave money and gifts to the couple, which she had planned to do in order to write thank you notes. But when she refused to share that list, her in-laws were furious, saying, "How do we know what to give to them (the wedding guests) later, if we don't know what they gave to you?"

Is it a "gift" if the donor believes that what was given should be paid back in equal measure? We may consider reciprocity an equitable solution to giving and receiving, but even the terminology indicates that there's an accounting on both sides. When we operate from a qualified need to give back something of equal or greater value, the desire to even the balance sheet diminishes the experience for both people.

Most people don't want to be called a "taker," with all of its negative connotations. It stems from a feeling of entitlement, a one-sided relationship that may offer immediate gratification, but eventually creates a stuck energy.

On the other hand, gracious receiving originates from a place of gratitude for the chance to connect at a deeper level. In order to fully and openly receive, we have to feel worthy. We also have to be willing to allow someone to give to us without the compulsion to even the score.

Ultimately, the value of a gift lies in what it represents —friendship, love, respect, and caring. When our giving and receiving derive from a source of joy, we create a balance and an equilibrium that is life-affirming.

Although at times, it's still uncomfortable to receive, for the most part I'm able now to switch roles with more ease and grace. I love experiencing an organic flow of generosity in my relationships. I've discovered when people give and receive with an open heart, without expectations, it circulates loving energy that everyone wants to be a part of.

Here are two stories about givers who were able to let go of their traditional roles in order to receive in a way that was enriching and empowering for everyone involved.

Remember Mike!

It's not quid pro quo ... it's flow.

Jo Mooy has always been a giver. One day, she learned a hard, but valuable lesson about the gift of receiving.

In her words, Jo shares how she got a new perspective on the flow of generosity, which she loves sharing with others:

"No, no, I can't accept that. It's too much. I can't let you do that!" One of the women had just given the other a most meaningful gift of true friendship. But the receiver would not allow herself to accept the generosity of her friend. I watched the interchange as the protests continued from one to the other. Seeing the impasse I stepped between them and offered this story to both of them:

After a year of searching, I had found a kitchen cabinet island that perfectly matched my granite kitchen counter tops. The online order was so heavy it had to be shipped to the local UPS store. I called Mike, the owner of the store, and told him to be on the lookout for it and to warn him that it weighed over 250 pounds. I also learned that the island cabinet had to be assembled so I asked Mike if he knew a handyman that could put it together for me. He didn't know of anyone so I figured I'd have to find one after the rolling cabinet was delivered.

About two weeks later, there was a knock at the front door. When I opened it, there was UPS Mike with the heavy shipment. But it wasn't in a shipping box; the cabinet had been assembled. Mike had rolled it up the driveway and wanted to place it in the kitchen for us. I was flabbergasted with what he'd done. Not only had he assembled the cabinet on his own time, but he had personally delivered it in his pickup truck.

I offered to pay Mike for his labor and effort but he refused. I insisted. He still refused, saying it was his way of helping his customers. Realizing he would not take any money, I went to a local restaurant and bought a gift card: dinner for two. Very proudly I went to the UPS store and gave it to Mike. He looked at the card, looked at me, and asked, "Why did you do that?" I said I wanted to show my appreciation. Mike said, "But in doing that you just diminished my gift to you." I felt about six inches tall.

When I told my friend that story, she got tears in her eyes and said she had never thought of a gift in that way before. I assured her that neither had I. But I always remembered what Mike had done and more importantly what he'd said about diminishing his gift. You see, Mike gave me much more than an assembled kitchen cabinet. He taught me the true meaning of gift-giving and gift-receiving. He taught me that it was okay to receive without one-upmanship. He taught me that the gift of the heart cannot be genuinely given unless there's a receiver willing to accept and allow the gift.

When you're next tempted to refuse or overcompensate for something that someone has done or a gift someone has given to you ... Remember Mike!

♡ *Do you have a balance of giving and receiving in your life?*

♡ *What do you do when someone does something kind for you?*

♡ *Have you ever felt a stuck energy in either your giving or your receiving?*

♡ *How can you create more of a flow*

The Art of Receiving

You are invited, in the next story, to witness someone's personal journey discovering the ebb and flow of life cycles, where roles are interchangeable and receptivity and appreciation are the best options:

Successful, savvy, and driven, Ramona was a raging extrovert who earned a high income in sales and marketing for major corporations. "I was all about people pleasing and proving that I was good enough, and I had the large mountain home and the newest vehicle to validate me," says Ramona. "My life was the stereotypical, corporate success story, where workaholism and perfectionism were glorified, while relationships and the needs of others were put on the back burner."

And then, in a little over a year, a series of losses began to shake up and to undermine Ramona's world. She was laid off from the job from which she had planned to retire. A large part of her nest egg disappeared in a bad real estate investment, followed by the biggest blow of all—a diagnosis of cancer.

There was the usual anger, denial, and fear: *How could I have cancer when I'm so strong and healthy? Why me?* Fortunately, Ramona had long ago taught herself to look for the gift in every situation. "The universe sent a huge intervention to make me stop. It was exactly what I needed," she says. "The process of chemo and radiation therapy stripped me down to the basics of life, forcing me to get in touch with and to take care of the real Ramona—the reflective and vulnerable one who had been carefully hidden for many years."

Throughout her life, Ramona had a reputation for being a giver. "Even as a young child, I took on the responsibility for the care of my four younger siblings when my parents weren't able to show up," she recalls. "People always saw me as strong and confident. It was difficult to switch roles, to be on the receiving end."

Often admired from a distance, Ramona's powerful presence made her seem somehow unapproachable. Yet, there was something special about Ramona to which people were drawn—a caring and engaging style of relating that made them like and trust her. When she allowed the shell to be chipped away, people couldn't seem to do enough to let her know how much she meant to them.

"It took being stripped down to the raw and ragged core to really take in that people cared about and wanted to be there for me," Ramona says. "Once I could get comfortable with it and feel that I was deserving of love, it felt good and gave me a whole new perspective on myself."

The Cross

Tamara was a fabric designer, who had met Ramona only a few times through a mutual friend. One of her favorite pieces, which she could never bring herself to sell, was an intricately detailed wall hanging of a cross. When Tamara learned of Ramona's illness, she came to visit, bringing with her this cherished piece of art. As she handed it to Ramona, Tamara said, "I know why I made this piece and who I made it for. There's no question in my mind that this was meant for you."

Ramona was deeply touched. In the past, she would have felt unworthy of accepting such a gift, and even now was tempted to return it when she felt better. But she came to realize that doing so would diminish the gift. *Tamara didn't make a mistake or feel sorry for me, she really wanted me to have this.*

Each time Ramona looks at the wall hanging, she's reminded of the joy that went into creating and giving it, and she feels loved.

Touchstone

Ramona is also allowing others in by her willingness to talk about her experiences and to share her vulnerability. She still has vivid memories of watching her own mother die of cancer without ever talking to Ramona about it. She's determined to authentically communicate her fears and anxieties, as well as to celebrate her strengths and successes.

One day, Ramona was working in her garden when Terri, a neighbor whom she rarely saw, happened to be on her deck and asked, "How are you?" "I couldn't pretend that I was doing fine," says Ramona. "As I started to tell her about my diagnosis I broke down crying, which was so unusual for me."

Terri quickly walked over to Ramona's place, the first time that she had ever been there, and put her arms around her. After a while, she asked Ramona if she would like to go to the rock shop, where she worked, to pick out a gift. Ramona had always had a fascination with rocks and minerals and thought it would be a fun diversion.

At the lapidary, Terri helped Ramona select three special rocks and minerals: covellite for healing, hematite for grounding and balance, and smoky quartz for releasing negative thoughts. Later, Ramona would carry these three minerals in her pocket and hold them during her chemo treatments, feeling their healing energy.

As they were walking out of the store, Terri pointed to a large piece of rose quartz, known for its heart calming energy. She wanted to purchase it for Ramona's garden, but Ramona said, "No, I want to pay for it myself." It had been easy accepting the three small pieces, but this was too much. Terri insisted on buying it for her, and once again Ramona got to experience absolute receiving, graciously accepting the gift of friendship and love. It was another touchstone during her journey of healing.

The Power Piece

Several weeks prior to her scheduled cancer treatment, Ramona and her partner, Liz, drove to a well-loved mountain town for a weekend getaway. They stopped in to their favorite jewelry store to say hello to the owner, whom they'd gotten to know over the years. Melanie, a skilled metals smith and jewelry designer, had just the day before put a premier piece that she had worked on for two years into a glass showcase.

"Try it on," suggested Liz, who was contemplating buying it for her.

It looked stunning on Ramona.

"How much is it?" asked Ramona.

"It's not for sale," said Melanie. "But do you really like it?"

"I love it!" said Ramona.

"Then I want you to have it," said Melanie. "I knew it belonged with you."

Ramona was speechless, not believing that someone would be so generous to her. Although she accepted the necklace, she couldn't sleep that night knowing that it was valued at close to $2,000, and that literally hundreds of hours had gone into hammering out each silver leaf. She decided to go back the next day to return it.

"It's gorgeous, but I just can't accept it," she said.

"Ramona, you've got to let me do this for you. I'd be hurt if you didn't accept it. It looks beautiful on you, and it's exactly what this piece was meant for," Melanie said. "Will you wear it during your treatments to give you strength?"

Ramona had only to look at Melanie to understand the joy that she was receiving from giving this gift.

In a flashback, Ramona remembered, at the age of eleven, being given $100 by her grandfather, a huge amount of money in those days. She was so excited she had asked for a ride to the jewelry store, where she purchased a gold necklace to surprise her mother. "It felt so good to see the joy on my mom's face. I loved her so much and was happy to find a way to show her."

During the ensuing weeks of chemo and radiation, Ramona wore her *power piece*, as she'd come to think of the necklace. Although she lost her hair and felt exhausted, she says, "the necklace made me feel beautiful and strong in the middle of a not very beautiful thing. It became an anchor for my feeling loved and cared about."

Now, months later, Ramona sometimes feels like she's living in limbo, uncertain what to do next. Living life at a slower pace has helped her to be fully present each moment and to explore what she really wants to do. "If this experience with cancer hadn't happened, I wouldn't be making the life choices I'm making now," says Ramona. Grateful for the loving support she has received on her journey of healing, she has also learned that "If I don't take care of myself first, I don't have the capacity to care for others."

While Ramona continues to be a generous giver, she also knows how to be a gracious and appreciative receiver, a full participant in the flow of love and friendship.

♡ *Reflect on a time when you were uncomfortable receiving a gift from someone, thinking that you would have to pay it back and not wanting to feel obligated.*

♡ *Imagine receiving that gift now with an open heart and appreciation for the person who simply wanted you to know that they cared.*

♡ *Give a gift today for the sheer joy of it, whether a physical or intangible expression of love or appreciation. Enjoy the good feelings that you experience from knowing that you brought unexpected pleasure to someone else.*

Unexpected Income

I first learned about the concept of giving 10 percent of "unexpected income" several years ago, during a course based on the teachings of Science of Mind. It offered a new and different twist on the practice of tithing.

During a ten-week period, we were asked to keep track of any "unexpected gifts or monies" that we received, and were invited to donate 10 percent of this unanticipated wealth. Each week we talked about what "showed up in our lives," and the appreciation that we felt. We then made a contribution to a charity we had mutually chosen. What we discovered was that when we were open to attracting abundance, it flowed naturally and easily to us. In a very short time, our group collected hundreds of dollars to give to those in need.

Throughout this process, I discovered numerous sources of unexpected income: A friend surprised me by treating me to lunch, a reduction was made in my bill, I got a refund for something that I didn't know about, a bank teller voluntarily made a recommendation that increased my profit, and I found money in the street ... and more.

The many forms of unexpected income that came to me supported my belief in a loving and plentiful universe. The more I looked for ways to participate in this flow of abundance, the more it continued to bless my life.

I've continued to embrace this practice. I've found it easy to be generous with money that I didn't have in my possession the day before, and it's fun to express my gratitude immediately.

Here are several examples of receiving unexpected monies and how they were put right back into circulation:

Once, I was stopped by a policeman for exceeding the speed limit. As I sat in my car, I put out a quick mental thought: *If this police officer doesn't give me a ticket, I will donate 10 percent of whatever the ticket would have been to charity.* The police officer returned with a citation, but said, "I could have given you a ticket for $115 MORE than what this citation will cost you." It was high but could have been almost double the amount and it had fewer points attached. When I got home, I noticed a request for donations from UNICEF. I immediately popped a fifteen dollar check in the mail to them, a little more than the 10 percent. I also paid my fine—more than $100—and made a decision to slow down the next time!

Two months ago, I went to a new chiropractor who had a charity fund-raising promotion. Instead of charging me the normal $120 as a new patient, I was charged only $25, which was then donated to the Red Cross. With gratitude, I made a donation of 10% of the savings to a different fund-raiser, for a family who had recently lost their home in a fire.

A local bank was about to charge a penalty fee of $91 for closing my CD early, and then decided not to penalize me. So, I gave $10 in cash to an organization that works on drop-out prevention for high school students.

I received a refund from my health insurance company,

shocked that they actually give money back. I chose to give a little over 10% of that refund to Kiva.org, which offers loans to individuals to start businesses and become self-sustaining. And an unexpected holiday gift gave me an opportunity to send a check to SAME Café, a non-profit restaurant, knowing that it would feed several people.

When I joyfully share the generosity that comes my way without expectations, I've learned it continues flowing to me … and thus to others. I love how that works.

♡ *What have you given away that has come back to you ten-fold?*

♡ *When do you feel most joyful about giving?*

♡ *If you won $10 million dollars, how would you spend it? How would you share it with others?*

The Ripple Effect

The Universe is a continuous web.
Touch it at any point and the web quivers.
– Stanley Kountz

Like the subtle waves in a pond, every thought and action creates a ripple effect. Even the simplest act can touch and inspire others in totally unexpected ways that we may never know about. Kindness is contagious and infectious, even when one isn't directly involved, but merely hears about the good deeds of others. Acts of love and kindness favorably affect not only the givers and receivers, but those who are witnesses.

Recurring Ripple
In the early stages of writing *Love Is the New Currency*, I enjoyed

sharing some of the stories with my friend, Tom Wentzel, who claims that he was "sworn to secrecy, under the threat of death" to keep this book under wraps. But right from the start, it had an effect on Tom, who says, "My volunteer spirit has been rekindled thanks to the stories I've read in your book and by your taking me to a local meeting of volunteers."

Here is how Tom chose to create his own unique ripple:

As a Florida Realtor, Tom knows that cash flow doesn't come readily during a real estate slump. Yet, he was so grateful for the steady growth of his new business and for the blessings in his life that he decided to take his entire stimulus check down to All Faiths Food Bank, a non-profit that provides more than 8,700 meals daily. Not only did Tom donate the $250 he had just received, but he matched it with his own savings to make a more substantial contribution.

As part of his commitment to a Sarasota volunteer group that we attended, Tom made a call to the volunteer coordinator of Big Brothers Big Sisters, and was so inspired by this woman's involvement that he decided to become a Big Brother. Thus began his relationship with fourteen-year-old Teddy. (As the father of three grown sons and one daughter, Tom brings a lot of expertise to the role.)

Another ripple occurred a few months later, when Tom stopped by with Teddy to visit a fellow Realtor, who was so impressed with Teddy that he, too, decided to become a Big Brother.

Teddy thrives on the attention he gets from Tom, and looks forward to each Saturday's rendezvous with his Big Brother. They have just celebrated their one-year mark and plan to continue for many more.

This was not the first time Tom responded to the call to make a difference. Growing up in a small town in Minnesota, Tom was fresh out of college when he signed up for two years with the Peace Corp in Swaziland, Africa. That decision ignited his altruistic and adventurous spirit. "While in Swaziland, I discovered many things that I had to share and yet, I always felt that no matter what I was able to give, I always received far more from the people that I was there to serve."

While in Africa, Tom took an interest in the life of his translator, Obed, a young boy of 12. In spite of Obed's limited resources, Tom saw his potential and helped him to get into a school run by the Selesian Brothers. Not only did Obed do exceptionally well, but with Tom's generosity and support, as well as with scholarship money, Obed went on to complete four years of college, followed by a master's degree in geology.

"Obed's more educated than I am," jokes Tom, with pride. Knowing that this might not have happened without his help, he says, "I am grateful that I was able to make a difference in just one person's life. Helping people is my legacy. I feel the best when I'm helping others."

♡ *If you knew that you couldn't fail, what would you be willing to do to positively influence someone's life?*

♡ *Is there a project to help others that you would want to get involved in if you had the time or money?*

♡ *Would you be willing to contribute an hour a week, and if not, an hour a month, if you knew that it would make a difference?*

Kindness Provides Warmth

A former Miss America beauty pageant contestant, Lisa Thole has the kind of warmth and openness that naturally draws people to her. As the volunteer coordinator at an elementary school where more than 85% of the children participate in the free and/ or reduced-price lunch program, Lisa is passionate about these children, especially those 200 students who are struggling with math and reading, members of the "Eagles Nest." She delights in seeing them succeed, becoming more loving towards themselves as they discover their self worth.

Here is how Lisa created a ripple of kindness when she noticed and met a need in the school community:

As Lisa stepped out of the classroom to walk across the school courtyard with Zoe, one of the students in her tutoring program, she noticed that the tiny five-year-old, dressed in a worn, spaghetti-strapped tank top, was shivering in the forty-degree temperature. "Where's your jacket?" Lisa asked. "Did you leave it in the classroom?"

Zoe shook her head: No.

"Did you leave it on the bus?"

The girl's long, dark braid moved from side to side.

"Did you leave it at home?" Again she received a negative, nonverbal response.

In disbelief, Lisa asked, "Do you have a jacket?"

Zoe shook her head once more and then looked down at the ground.

Lisa immediately took off her own jacket and wrapped it around Zoe. She couldn't imagine a child not having a jacket in cold weather.

Upon investigation, she learned that the girl was one of eight siblings living with their grandmother. With limited funds of her own, Lisa went out that day and purchased two children's coats. She'd decided to give one to Zoe and to have an extra one on hand "just in case it happened again."

Then, Lisa began to notice many more kids at school without jackets. She asked the teachers if they could send her a list of names of those students who consistently came in without coats, and she was shocked to get more than one hundred children's names from thirty different teachers.

That night, at a book club meeting, Lisa started to cry as she shared this story. One member, Ginny, suggested, "Why don't you start a jacket fund?"

"How?" Lisa asked.

Ginny replied, "You just start one!"

And so it began.

Seed money to start the fund was donated by some members of her club, followed by a consistent flow of cash and coats from the volunteers at the school, friends, and friends of friends. Like so many great ideas, her vision took on a life of its own as others were moved to participate.

Lisa was amazed by the generosity of people who went out and bought brand-new coats. Every day, the office would call and there would be another bag of coats waiting, purchased by total strangers who were also likely to be experiencing tough economic times, and could have used the money for their own children or grandchildren.

She personally handled the distribution of the coats. One by one, a child would be invited to Lisa's room and given a warm, well-fitting jacket. "Each face would light up with a huge smile," says Lisa. "They were so appreciative. It was as if the jacket gave them a message that they were loved, that someone thought that they were special. For many, the fact that the jackets were brand new was like winning the lottery. They walked out of the room ten inches taller."

One volunteer, Dee, had noticed a tag sticking out of one little girl's coat and said, "Let me get the scissors to cut that off."

"No," the little girl pleaded, and Dee realized just how proud she was of her first store-bought jacket.

"The experience of people caring about other people's children fills me with tremendous hope for humanity," says Lisa. "It also gives me peace of mind, knowing that these children won't be cold."

"I love my work," Lisa adds. "I see magic everyday in the interactions between adult volunteers and our eager and grateful students. It's inspiring to witness young children learning to believe in themselves and making breakthroughs in academics."

Although Lisa never asks directly for donations, she's always amazed at how many people come forward to help, once they know that there's a genuine need.

At one party just before the holidays, a man whom she'd just met asked Lisa about her job. After she told him about the children at her school, he said, "What would you do with twenty-one bicycles if they just dropped out of thin air? Could you find a home for them?"

"I can find a home for them faster than you can blink an eye," she replied. And so it was that brand-new bikes, along with helmets and locks, were secretly delivered to the school just in time for the holidays. The teachers helped to choose twenty-one of the neediest students, and called their parents to come to the school's side door to pick one up.

Lisa recalls the tears in the eyes of one large man, who was so surprised to be handed a new bike that he could never have afforded. Like so many of the parents, he was grateful to be able to make his child's Christmas special.

Coats to Books

The coat drive created more ripples…

Sandy Caplan, Sally Gabriel, and a team of campaign volunteers were inspired by President Barack Obama's message inviting people to get involved in their community.

Sandy had been tutoring kindergarten students when she heard about Lisa's jacket drive. Not only did she, Sally, and their team collect coats, hats, and mittens, they decided to adopt the school, where the majority of the 700 students were from low income families. After meeting with the principal, assistant principal, and Lisa to determine the greatest need, they were told: "Most of these children do not own even one book or have books available in their homes. Many of the families don't speak English."

"Our goal was to collect one new book for each of the 700

elementary students," says Sandy. "We posted signs in our housing developments, talked to book stores, put notices in the paper, and sent out e-mails. We were stunned by the results." Their community effort netted about 4,000 books!

The volunteers sorted all the books by grade level, and the fifth-graders helped to deliver them to the classrooms. The kids were thrilled. Some of the children received as many as seven new or gently used books. They read their books on the last day of school, and then took them home to read again over the summer.

The third ripple came a year later when Lisa spearheaded the Book Buddy Project, an innovative reading program to promote literacy year-round. "We wanted to provide each of our 200 Eagle's Nest students with a book bag, three books, and a fuzzy, cuddly teddy bear, who would be a "book buddy" for the children to read to throughout the summer," says Lisa. Once again, the generosity of numerous volunteers was astounding.

At last count, they had collected 202 bears, 533 books and $1,040 in monetary donations.

And knowing Lisa, the ripple will continue.

♡ *How can you share your warmth and kindness more frequently and perhaps in a new way with others?*

♡ *What could you do to seed an idea that will generate its own loving flow of energy?*

♡ *What would it feel like to be a part of a larger ripple that would positively affect others?*

Eleven
111 Expressions
of Everyday Kindness

In this life, we cannot do great things,
we can only do small things with great care.

—Mother Teresa

Some are simple, while others may seem grander, but each gesture of love, respect, and consideration has an immeasurable value, both to the giver and to the recipient. You're invited to witness these 111 individual acts of kindness, and to allow them to be catalysts, inciting you to create and express your own *currency of love.*

♡ While Art was enjoying his coffee, at a restaurant off of the highway not far from where he lived, he noticed a family who was stranded because their car had broken down. Without hesitation, Art offered to drive them home—a full hour away!

♡ Peter and his daughter, Jessica spend their Christmas Eve wrapping presents that they have previously purchased for local migrant workers, and then deliver them on Christmas day.

♡ Linda can't walk by someone who is taking a picture of their friends or family without offering to take the photo so that their visual memories will include everyone.

♡ When Margaret realized that a friend needed a haircut but couldn't afford one, she invited the woman into her home and cut her hair herself.

♡ John rides his bicycle everywhere, collecting trash that he sees on his travels and picking up any useable clothes or items, which he then takes to charity drop-offs.

♡ A manager at an upscale restaurant, Stefan purchases hundreds of angel pins and gives out at least one a day to customers whom he feels could use a "lift" or a blessing.

♡ Christine volunteers as a "cuddler" at the local neonatal intensive care unit, feeding, changing, and holding newborns.

♡ A busy psychotherapist, Jessie spent forty hours to become certified to handle hazardous waste, so that she could volunteer to clean shorebirds oiled in the recent Gulf Oil spill.

♡ Nine-year old Jenny made a very special request on her birthday: Instead of presents, she asked that donations be made to a local animal shelter, raising hundreds of dollars.

♡ When Sam, a street person, noticed a woman who looked unhappy, he used his index fingers to lift both corners of his mouth, creating an exaggerated smile. He then did a wheelie in his wheel chair to make her laugh.

♡ Sue, Bob, and their three sons—Matt, age six, Todd, age eight, and Alex, age twelve—donate some of their family time on Christmas morning to serve food at a local shelter.

♡ Jim and Meghan spent their first week of married life "honeyteering" in another state, where they helped to build a home for a needy family through Habitat for Humanity.

♡ Sara collects cans and bottle tops for money, which she brings to her favorite local charity.

♡ Van takes a friend, who is blind, grocery shopping and out for walks, patiently helping him to adjust and learn about his new living environment.

♡ Ten year old Kris, was upset to see the devastating results of a tornado in a nearby town. With his Mom's help, he bought food, water, and snacks and delivered them to many displaced kids and adults.

♡ At the end of each yoga class, Charley picks up the yoga blocks of the person(s) nearby, as he puts his own away. As a result, those who have experienced the kindness have turned around and done the same for another person.

♡ When Trent meets someone who has something that needs repair, he helps them to fix it, and then spends the time to teach them how to do it themselves in the future.

♡ A former Las Vegas nightclub singer, Altazar finds joy singing at nursing homes and retirement centers. He loves seeing the Alzeimer's patients light up when he croons familiar Frank Sinatra songs.

♡ Every day Murray looks for someone or something to say "YES" to. He gives at least a dollar a day to whomever he encounters who needs something—whether it is a street person asking for change or a fund-raising event.

♡ Tomas often puts money in parking meters that are about to expire. With the new meter-less pay parking system, he now takes his ticket if it has unused time on it, and either hands it to someone or places it on their windshield.

♡ While Erik was in line at a local sandwich shop, the woman in front of him kept swiping her credit card to no avail. She had no cash and turned to walk away from the food that she'd just ordered, when Erik said, "Hey, I've got cash. Let me pay for that!"

♡ Tim, who once lived at a homeless shelter, now volunteers there to fix any bicycles that have been donated.

♡ Every month Adrianne buys bags full of nonperishable food and brings it to the local food bank.

♡ Eddy and his buddies bring their grills to the local baseball games, where they sell hamburgers to raise money for shelters and charities in their community.

♡ Deborah expresses love and appreciation daily by sending unexpected, personalized, and uplifting greeting cards to friends, family, business associates, and those in need of cheer.

♡ During a neighbor's first and second deployment to Iraq, Patrick mowed this man's lawn to help the family who was left behind.

♡ When family members or friends are experiencing difficult or unstable life situations, Beth will pick them up and bring them to her home for the day, providing lunch, letting them do their laundry, and giving them a respite from their challenging lives.

♡ JoeJoe brings leftover food from his catering events to local shelters. He has gotten so popular with the men at these shelters that when he arrives, they jump up and down doing a rap version of *"Hey, it's the man with the cheese!"*

♡ Geoffrey could hardly wait to turn eighteen so that he could become a "cat cuddler" at the local animal shelter. He often brings in clean, used towels so that the cats have something comfortable to lie on.

♡ As a retiree, Susan treasures her time tutoring two first graders in reading, twice a week. She recently accepted one more challenging student because she believes in the school's philosophy of "no child left behind."

♡ Laurie, who once worked as a chamber maid, always cleans the hotel room that she is vacating, taking off the sheets and emptying the trash, to make it easier on those whose job it is to clean up after others.

♡ And Arthur always leaves the biggest tips for chamber maids because he says, "They have the toughest job!"

♡ When going through the checkout line at the grocery store, George makes it a point to ask his cashier how her/his day is going before paying for his groceries and walking away.

♡ For the last three years, Lori has been facilitating free weekly writer's group meetings to create a supportive community for local authors.

♡ Seeing a dejected-looking homeless man, Todd asked him if he was hungry. When the man said "yes," Todd went to a nearby market to buy him a healthy sandwich.

♡ Lenore never hesitates to open her wallet when she notices that someone in line in front of her doesn't have the right amount of change.

♡ Gary carries a hundred-dollar bill folded and tucked in his wallet. He has given it away three different times to someone who needed it more than he did.

♡ Joni hosts monthly healing sessions, where members of the community can receive free massage, energy work or any number of services offered by health professionals.

♡ One volunteer in her eighties, Corinne loves facilitating

people's healing process by using an energy technique to diagnose health problems and recommend natural remedies.

♡ Knowing that doves mate forever, John was saddened to see one hit by a car. As its partner continued to fly into traffic, John jumped out of his car, and moved the dead dove to the side of the road to keep the other one safe.

♡ Steve loves sharing his seva (service) practice, which he does by being a pen pal—writing regularly to two inmates in prison.

♡ Tony and Tyler jointly raised more than $17,000 as part of AIDS LifeCycle—a seven day, 545-mile "bike ride of love" from San Francisco to Los Angeles that generated more than $10 million to support disease awareness, prevention, and treatment.

♡ When Don noticed that his down sleeping bag had a broken zipper, he had it dry-cleaned and brought it to a local shelter, where it was gratefully accepted as a warm blanket.

♡ Elizabeth's community service is keeping a popular beach area that she frequents clean and free of trash.

♡ Whenever Teresa leaves work on a snowy day, she secretly brushes the snow off of the car of her older co-worker who is not in good health.

♡ Nineteen year old Amanda greets people with a big smile, especially those who look sad. She always acknowledges and holds the door open for others.

♡ To create a better experience for his neighbors living in a condo complex, Meredith purchased two garden benches, placing them in tranquil settings for others to enjoy.

♡ Jamie is committed to recycling as a way to positively impact her environment. She picks up used papers from the elderly, and has been seen going through the postal service trash, looking for tossed magazines and newspapers to bring to the recycling center.

♡ Stephanie goes out of her way to acknowledge people who give good service, sometimes writing and sending letters of recommendation to managers or corporate headquarters.

♡ In a neighborhood of growing families, Kate, a young mom, helps her neighbors by watching their kids in a pinch or by sharing the fruits of her garden.

♡ Doug, who works at a large corporation, secretly leaves presents and gift baskets for several of his co-workers who are single moms, making them feel special and cared for.

♡ When dining out, Terry stacks the used plates and utensils to make it easier for the wait staff. At fast-food restaurants, she completely clears her table, leaving it clean and inviting for the next person.

♡ Johnny ventures out in major snow storms with his snow blower and shovel to dig out his elderly neighbors.

♡ Even in a highly populated condo complex, people experience loneliness within their walls. Leslie stopped by to visit a single elderly neighbor, and later took her to a nearby senior center so that she could meet other people.

♡ Russell and Rita have an open door policy, sharing their lovely home with those in need. Most recently the person mowing their lawn was going through a divorce and needed a place to stay for a few weeks. He became a welcomed guest for four months!

♡ In her mid-twenties and unable to find a job, Judy loves volunteering as a Pop Warner coach for eight to ten year old cheerleaders.

♡ Whenever a rude driver cuts her off in traffic or impatiently honks their horn at her, Mo returns this negative action with a positive gesture—her warm smile and a friendly wave.

♡ Through a program called "Decisions to Win," Rebecca, a fashion consultant, mentors at-risk high school students weekly, teaching self-confidence and good decision making skills ... and has done so for four years.

♡ Knowing how difficult it can be to be a newcomer, Linda Rae takes it upon herself to greet and welcome new faces, whether at a church or social gathering. She has even been known to walk down the street, smiling and greeting strangers as she walks by them.

♡ Maureen and Paul spent sixteen long hours trimming trees and mulching to help a widow on their mountain top. When she offered to pay them, they simply smiled and said, "We don't charge neighbors."

♡ A successful plumber, Ron donates a percentage of everything that he makes to a favorite charity voted on by his clients.

♡ Joyce purchases Boulder Bucks, a regional currency good at local supermarkets, gas stations, and public transportation, which she hands out to street people instead of cash.

♡ Annie and her husband, Jerry, are successful electricians, who donated 60 hours to rewire their mountain community center making it safer for its members. In the past, Annie and some of her students volunteered to wire twelve Habitat for Humanity homes.

♡ Jon volunteers to refurbish old computers through a local nonprofit, then delivers and sets them up in the homes of those who are disabled.

♡ Roberto expresses his kindness while he's driving, letting people cut in or allowing them to pass, to make it a less stressful experience.

♡ Whenever Marie notices an attendant sweeping the floors or cleaning the sinks in an airport restroom, she hands her a dollar saying, "Thank you for keeping it clean for us."

♡ An animal lover, Ellen not only adopts dogs that are difficult to find homes for, but also takes in older dogs that no one wants. She spends a great deal of time and money to ensure that the dogs have good health, as well as a loving home.

♡ Peg and her husband, Don, regularly go through their closets, looking for clothes they no longer wear. They personally bring them to a homeless shelter, where they know they'll get used immediately.

♡ At graduation time, Maya loans her cap and gown each year to a student who can't afford to rent or buy one.

♡ Karen uses humor to get people to open up and smile ... or most often to laugh.

♡ Verna teaches English to immigrants from many different parts of the world to help them adjust to their new home in the United States.

♡ Yvonne visits a nearby nursing home regularly to cheer up the residents. She loves to bring her home-cooked Vietnamese food for them to enjoy.

♡ A wildlife and scenic photographer, Susan often donates her framed photographs to charity auctions, particularly those focused on saving and protecting wildlife.

♡ When a man behind her in a long grocery line kept looking at his watch, Dana let him get in front of her so that he could get to his destination sooner.

♡ When someone whom she cares about passes away, Kay plants a tree in their honor.

♡ No matter how busy he is, Bob offers a helping hand when needed. He says, "I do things for others because it's who I am. I treat a stranger the same way I treat a friend."

♡ On a recent flight, Jeff noticed that the young boy next to him was distraught because his DVD player wasn't working. Without hesitation, Jeff handed over his computer so that he could watch his movies. (Now that probably provided an instant payback!)

♡ Acknowledging that there is a real person trying to make a living on the other end of the solicitation phone calls, Carol politely expresses that she's not interested and thanks them before hanging up.

♡ Louise is a connector who generously shares contacts and resources to help others.

♡ Paula keeps an eye out for elderly neighbors or those who have handicaps, offering to help them as needed. She also volunteers in the kitchen at her place of worship.

♡ Although she was born with a profound hearing loss, Darlene had a successful business career. In her spare time, she mentors deaf high school students, encouraging them to get good grades and to apply to college, so they can compete in the professional job market.

♡ At a local park—an unofficial gathering place for the "homeless," Virginia and other volunteers prepare and bring individually wrapped meals, to share food and fellowship.

♡ For their annual Christmas gift exchange, a group of 12 Colorado business women chose to combine the money they would have spent on presents, and donate it to a charity. They then selected a book from their own bookshelf, wrapped it, and brought it to exchange.

♡ On the rare occasions that Marie cooks, she makes sure that her older neighbors on both sides of her get to enjoy a home-cooked meal, too.

♡ Ben took his "empty nest"—three bedrooms vacated by his sons—and opened it up to people in need: a neighbor who had a flooded basement, a friend who lost his job, and another friend who suffered some financial setbacks.

♡ One hot day, a woman with a toddler in a carriage was exhausted as she walked to the entrance of the Wellness Fair, only to realize that she had forgotten her wallet at home. One of the volunteers readily handed her $5 to pay the entrance fee.

♡ John, Theo, Brennan, Phil, and Kati had a sign offering FREE HUGS outside of a music festival, and got lots of willing recipients.

♡ Michael knows the name of every bank teller, store clerk, receptionist, or waiter of any business that he frequents. They light up when he greets them by name

♡ The gift of music is what Roger loves to share as he brings his guitar to serenade the elderly at assisted-living centers.

♡ As she was downsizing for a move, instead of a yard sale, Nicky invited friends over to select from the things she was letting go of, and if they chose, to make a donation. In this way, Nicky collected more than $1,000 for a local charity, and her friends got to enjoy new treasures for their homes.

♡ Joe can't go hiking without his picking up at least ten or twenty things—soda cans, cigarette butts, bottle tops—discarded on the mountain trails.

♡ Dudley believes that kind words and the gift of presence can make someone's day. Now that he is retired, he regularly visits those in convalescent centers and on life care, and simply sits and talks with them.

♡ Doc, as he is known to the residents of a homeless shelter, is a retired doctor in his late eighties. Although he is unsteady on his feet, he volunteers to wash laundry, as well as to assist in the temporary clinic.

♡ After she finishes reading a good book, Ellen leaves it wherever she happens to be—on a park bench, on a bus, at a café—knowing that the person who picks it up is exactly who should read it next.

♡ To benefit her coastal environment, Verna walks the beach at daybreak for the turtle patrol. Locating and marking a turtle nest might mean that more than one hundred baby turtles will have a chance of survival.

♡ One day a week, Angela visited a home for the blind, where volunteers were matched with a resident and asked to read whatever was requested. Her "match" was a muscular young man who loved having her read the latest edition of a magazine for bodybuilders.

♡ At nine years old, Leo is so compassionate that he refuses to join his friends in making fun of a girl in his class who looks "weird" because she has seizures. Not only did he stand up to his friends, but he spoke to the principal about it.

♡ Every year, despite the demands of his real estate business, Ed brings family members, friends from his company and community, as well as people he's never met before, to Juarez, Mexico, for two days to build homes for families in need of a place to live.

♡ Susan loves to sew for single mothers and their newborns, as well as to create personalized items for the elderly. She also sews for the sailors who are temporarily docked in her town.

♡ As a hair stylist, Sue Anne's passion is making people feel beautiful. Every Wednesday for three years, she volunteered to cut hair for residents of a local homeless shelter.

♡ The peaceful sounds of Diana's flute provide comfort, whether people are attending a memorial service, hospice's celebration of life, or one of many community gatherings.

♡ When Lynne's next door neighbor was diagnosed with stomach cancer, Lynne considered it an honor to take care of her—washing, bathing, and feeding her daily.

♡ Danielle brings the discount coupons that she gets in the mail to the stores, where she gives them to someone about to make a purchase. It has made several people happy.

♡ Paul has developed the habit of donating his blood, a pint at a time, for more than thirty years. Twice he was acknowledged as a member of the "Two Gallon Club," and has given about six gallons since he started.

♡ Martina brought towels that she no longer used to a day center for the homeless, where they would be used by the many guests who showered there.

♡ As part of their church's focus on community service, Tyler and Tony participate in the Student-Run Free Clinic, where medical students and volunteers provide health and social services to people without insurance or access to medical care.

♡ For three years, Sally has been a board member of a non-profit organization that houses and feeds homeless families and helps them to find jobs. She also organizes fund raisers to support these efforts.

♡ A sophomore in high school, Max volunteers at the local senior center to teach an older generation how to use technology and be more connected in their limited worlds.

♡ Tajali brings the Dances of Universal Peace to schools, where at-risk children can learn to see and acknowledge the beauty in everyone, including themselves.

♡ Linda Rae is a "Faith Angel." Along with other members

of her church group, she volunteers to prepare and deliver home-cooked meals to those who have had a death in their family, undergone surgery, had a new baby or are in need of assistance.

♡ During the Christmas holiday, Dee creates 200 stockings and fills them with goodies to distribute to needy children.

Epilogue

The writing of *Love Is the New Currency* took on a life of its own. In fact, it has been very much, I'm told, like birthing a baby. Seven months ago, (after 18 months of writing), when I thought the book was "almost" finished, I was pushing to have it completed before the holidays. A friend, Nance, sat me down and said, "Linda, natural childbirth is a much better way to go than using forceps." It was then I decided to birth this book at a slower, more natural pace.

Some people couldn't understand how it could take so long, like my dad, for example. Typically, when I called to talk with him, he would ask, "So, what's new?" I'd say, "Well, Dad, the book is almost finished." And he'd reply, "I said, 'What's new?'"

If there were times when writing this book felt like a daunting task, the face of one of the story tellers or their words of gratitude for the chance to share a part of their lives would come to mind and would rouse me from the throes of "writer's block" to keep me going, one sentence and one story at a time.

And then there was the issue of FLOW! Having a "Type A" personality, I habitually set writing deadlines. I would sit at my desk and say, "Ok, I'm ready to go with the flow now"—NOW being the operative word. Often, I couldn't meet my writing goals (at least not with anything you'd want to read), and it took me a while to realize that writing a book and birthing a baby don't work that way—they have their own timing. Besides, I was committed to making this the very best book that I could, no matter how long it took. And the discipline to sit there and keep at it, even when I wasn't in the flow, did pay off.

It was like working on a jigsaw puzzle. I felt overwhelmed at first, when I couldn't yet see the big picture and how it would come together. But synchronistically, piece by piece, story by story, it did, and I saw a beautiful picture: a world that looked kinder and more loving than what the local and world news would have me see.

My journey to find hope and meaning during these challenging times has been a life-changing experience. Today, I'm more positive, peaceful, and secure. I like to think I'm more patient and understanding, more accepting of myself and others. As I open my heart to connect more deeply with others, I trust that I am living in a friendly universe. I find myself looking forward to meeting new people, listening to their stories, and discovering how they are defining and expressing their *currency of love*.

Each time someone shares their heartfelt experience with me, I'm aware that I am being given a precious gift. As the "witness," listening to and later writing down their story, my energy is elevated. I feel good. What I've discovered is that with each kind act, there is not only a huge energetic benefit for the receiver and the giver, but for anyone who gets to be a witness, too. It has been my intention, in writing *Love Is the New Currency*, to share these uplifting accounts in a way that will bring the same good feelings to those who read them.

Oftentimes, the storytellers were humble, reticent at first to talk about the things they'd done. I felt like I was on a treasure hunt—searching for the "heart of gold," which I believe is in everyone. And I wanted to hold on to and cherish these stories, as I have my grandfather's silver dollars.

Each story I've heard has changed me in some way, especially in how I see and relate to people and their circumstances. There was a time when I would have been impressed with others' financial success and accumulation of wealth, but I see now that each of us, regardless of our financial situation, has something precious to share, a *currency of love,* that increases the more we give it away.

Measuring wealth in this way allows us to be equal participants in the flow of abundance, as givers and receivers. When we experience our commonality, our deep connection, we know that we're not alone.

In fact, I've always believed that none of us should ever feel like we're alone, which is why I've always been a "connector." I was once told that I was like an old-fashioned switchboard operator, who would plug in calls, opening lines of communications to bring people together and to share resources. It's my way of creating a measure of wealth that has nothing to do with money and everything to do with the *currency of love*. Writing this book has fed that passion and has provided a perfect forum to introduce people who inspire others to make a difference and to spread the seeds of kindness.

Even one act of kindness can be so contagious that its ripple effect can go on indefinitely, touching others in unanticipated, often extraordinary, ways. When we can see the ripple effects that come from giving, and can savor and enjoy the benefits over time, we realize that the good that we do does matter.

I've learned that giving in the moment, when the need is immediate has a far more profound effect than giving at years-end or simply for tax purposes. When we give throughout the year, we address needs as they arise and there is more time to create ongoing ripples of kindness. In fact, in the past two years, although I still give to organizations, I am quicker to open my wallet to help others directly, giving more to people that I know personally who are having a hard time.

If you are like me, you hunger for "good news"—for proof that kindness is still abundant in the world, that generosity and compassion are innate qualities that define the human heart. Collecting these stories and meeting such kind and generous people has made me much more hopeful that together we can create a world that works well for everyone.

I wrote *Love Is the New Currency* as an expression of gratitude and a celebration of the human spirit. It's a journey that continues to unfold and I invite you to come along. We all have so much to offer, so many ways to create our own "kindness ripples," that make a positive difference in the lives of others. We can begin where we are, with small acts of kindness and grow our "wealth" from there. We can ask ourselves: What is my *currency of love*, and how can I circulate it and share it with others?

The world is shifting and so are we. It is my hope that *Love Is the New Currency*, not only inspires you to step into the shift consciously, but empowers you to create a world that is friendly, loving, kind, and connected – one in which we can all participate.

As Rabbi Hillel so poignantly asked: "If not now, when?" Let's not wait another moment.

♡ *What is one thing that you can do today to make someone's life better?*

♡ *What kind of world do you envision and what are you willing to do to create it?*

♡ *Would you be willing to share what actions you take as a result of reading this book so that others can be inspired, too?*

If you're open to sharing your personal stories, reflections, or insights, please consider putting them on the web site: www.loveisthenewcurrency.com

Thank you, Linda

All you need is love.
— The Beatles

Gratitudes

I am grateful for each person who supported me on this incredible journey of writing *Love Is the New Currency*.

Heartfelt thanks to Linda Maree, for her loving dedication, her invaluable editing, and for encouraging me to dig deeper for the core essence of each story; Louise Aveni, for nurturing my vision and coaching me through the creation of my first book; Lori DeBoer, for her insightful editing and gentle coaxing to find and express my voice; Sonya Hemmings, for her beautifully polished edits; Michael Healy, for his support and guidance in finding the common thread that weaves the stories together; Nance Warner, for validating my vision and encouraging me to birth this book at a slower, more natural pace; Tony Dylan-Hyde, for helping me to successfully navigate the world of trademarks; Mark Carson, for his financial advice and support of this project; Andrea Costantine, for teaching me effective marketing techniques; and Andrew Young, for generously sharing his marketing expertise.

A special "thank you" to the many friends who believe in *Love Is the New Currency* and have offered their input on this artistic journey: Peter Cohn, Liz Hafer, Diana Keck, Carol Kelly, Stephanie Kelso, Paula Montana, Joyce Paulin-Platek, Susan and Roger Peirce, Adie and David Rubin, Laurel Rund, Teresa Summers, Tajali Tolan, Bob Waters, Tom Wentzel, Jessie Williams, Tom Wilson, and Rachelle Zola. I truly appreciate each of them and feel blessed to have these friends in my life.

I am eternally grateful to Art and Terry Commito for being such wonderful parents and for their unwavering belief in me. I wouldn't be the person that I am without their love and support. A special thank you to my brothers, Robert and Tyler, for their friendship, and for being great role models for how to treat people with respect and kindness.

And my deepest appreciation goes to the amazing people who openly shared their heart-centered stories, and offered inspiring examples of how to create a kinder, more loving world. They are what *Love Is the New Currency* is all about.

Ways to Share Your Generosity

Please consider making donations to the organizations found in this book and listed below.

Marshall Direct Fund
P.O. Box 4477
Aspen, Co. 81612
970-963-3150
www.marshalldirectfund.org
Provides education and meals for impoverished children in Pakistan.

ShelterBox USA
8374 Market St. #203
Lakewood Ranch, Fl 34202
(941) 907-6036
www.shelterboxusa.org
Provides shelter, warmth and dignity to survivors of natural and man-made disasters around the world.

SourcePoint Global Outreach
Neil Steven Cohen / Executive Director
Tel: (831) 459-7684, (877) 277-6075
www.sourcepointglobaloutreach.org
Solar Light Project
Provides solar powered flashlights to humanitarian organizations and to villages in developing countries without adequate lighting.

So All May Eat, Inc.
SAME Cafe
2023 E. Colfax Ave.
Denver, CO 80206
720-530-6853
www.soallmayeat.org
Offers healthy meals on a pay-as-you-can basis.

Brothers and Sisters Doing the Right Thing
c/o North Sarasota Public Library
2801 Newtown Blvd.
Sarasota, Florida 34234
Benefits low income children and teens.

CharityFocus
http://charityfocus.org/donate or checks can be mailed to:
CharityFocus
P.O. Box 2711
Santa Clara, CA 95055
Supports a range of "gift economy" projects, including Karma Kitchen.

The following charitable organizations are not in the book, but are making a huge difference by helping people to become self-sufficient:

Heifer International
www.Heifer.org
(800) 422-0474
Provides livestock, seeds, or training to families struggling with hunger and poverty.

Kiva
www.Kiva.org
Makes microcredit loans in $25 increments to support small business ventures in becoming self-sustaining.
(As the loans are paid back, you are able to re-loan the funds.)

Thank you for your support.

Recommendations

The following books have inspired me prior to, or on, this journey of writing *Love Is the New Currency*:

The Book of Awakening by Mark Nepo

The Compassionate Life by Marc Ian Barasch

A New Earth by Eckhart Tolle

Soul of a Citizen by Paul Rogat Loeb

The Power of Kindness by Piero Ferrucci

The Power of Serving Others by Gary Morsch and Dean Nelson

The Soul of Money by Lynne Twist

Inspirational website:

One World Heart Project
http://owhp.org
Creates opportunities for everyday people to inspire positive change in the world. Dedicated to spreading the message that "Making a World of Difference" is simple and fun.

Here are some great websites that offer daily uplifting messages:

www.dailygood.org

www.helpothers.org

www.karmatube.org

www.ijourney.org

Also, check out www.loveisthenewcurrency.com to read other uplifting comments and stories, as well as to write about your own experiences of creating kindness ripples and expressing your *currency of love.*

Please consider submitting your stories for future editions of *Love Is the New Currency.*

About the Author

Linda Commito grew up in New England. After receiving her B.A. in English from Stonehill College, she spent her early career as an elementary school teacher, before taking on other roles and experiences that have enriched her life: author, entrepreneur, consultant and facilitator.

Linda's passion for connecting people was integral to the success of her businesses:

Commito and Company, a wholesale manufacturer's representative firm, specializing in high quality home accessories and gift lines, brought together committed sales reps with innovative retailers and interior designers in the Rocky Mountain states. Fifteen years later, Linda sold that company, which continues to do well.

She then created and facilitated *CommitoConnections,* a supportive, interactive, and enriching community for successful women business owners, for more than seven years.

Now, through *Love Is the New Currency,* a beautiful collection of inspirational, heart-centered stories, Linda is fulfilling a part of her dream to make a positive contribution to the planet and leave this world a kinder, more loving, and interconnected place.

CPSIA information can be obtained at www.ICGtesting.com

228594LV00003B/2/P

9 780984 446803